Pay Less Property Tax 2007

Tax busting tips to help boost your property profits!

By

Arthur Weller & Amer Siddiq

Publisher Details
This guide is published by Tax Portal Ltd. PO Box 844, Warrington, WA5 3ZT

'Pay Less Property Tax' – First published in December 2004.

Second Edition June 2005, Third Edition April 2006

A CIP Copy of this book is available from the British Library

ISBN 0-9549347-7-6

Disclaimer

1. This guide is produced for General guidance only, and professional advice should be sought before any decision is made. Individual circumstances can vary and therefore no responsibility can be accepted by the author, Arthur Weller, or the publisher Tax Portal Ltd, for any action taken, or any decision made to refrain from action, by any readers of this guide.

2. Tax rules and legislation are constantly changing and therefore the information printed in this guide is correct at the time of printing – April 2006.

3. Neither the author nor Tax Portal Ltd offer financial, legal or investment advice. If you require such advice then, we urge you to seek the opinion of an appropriate professional in the relevant field. We care about your success and therefore encourage you to take appropriate advice before you put any of your financial or other resources at risk. Don't forget, investment values can decrease as well as increase.

4. To the fullest extent permitted by law, Arthur Weller and Tax Portal Ltd do not accept liability for any direct, indirect, special, consequential or other losses or damages of whatsoever kind arising from using this guide.

   The guide itself is provided 'as is' without express or implied warranty.

5. Arthur Weller and Tax Portal Ltd reserve the right to alter any part of this guide any time without notice

Contents

About the Authors

Some words about the authors of this unique guide, bringing together a property tax specialist and a property investor!

Arthur Weller - The Property Tax Specialist

Arthur Weller is a tax specialist who advises other accountants. He is one of the most knowledgeable and respected tax specialists in the country.

He is also the lead technical tax specialist and design consultant for www.property-tax-portal.co.uk.

Arthur is based in the northwest and qualified in 1997 as a certified accountant in a small firm of accountants. They specialised to a degree in property, and he worked for some years in their tax department.

He then moved on to a medium-sized firm, where he was the technical manager in the tax department.

In 1998 he passed the exams of the Institute of Taxation, and in June 2000 he left to set up his own tax consultancy.

Arthur works mainly in an advisory capacity for accountants in all areas of taxation. He also runs a telephone help line, giving phone advice on all areas of taxation to accountants around the country.

Much of his work has been focused in the following areas:

- property taxation (Arthur is regarded as a property tax specialist);
- capital gains tax;
- stamp duty;
- income tax;
- company tax;
- tax repercussions of going abroad;
- tax investigations and generally dealing with the Inland Revenue.

Arthur has also written tax guidance articles.

Amer Siddiq - The Property Investor

Amer Siddiq is the founder of www.property-tax-portal.co.uk, a Web site dedicated to helping property investors pay less in property taxes!

He is passionate about all aspects of property investment and over the last six years has grown a portfolio in the northwest of England.

Amer is also a public speaker and regularly gives talks at the Property Investor Show.

He has also written much-sought-after property investment reports.

Acknowledgements

Ian McTernan, Tax Specialist and author of 'How to use Companies to cut your property tax bills', for contributing tax expertise and content to this guide.

Alistair Davidson, Tax Specialist. He is the personal accountant and tax advisor for Amer Siddiq, and has helped Amer to build his property tax knowledge.

Daniel Feingold, International Law and Tax Specialist. Daniel is a rarity amongst tax specialists as not only is he a much sought after international tax specialist but he is also a barrister (NP). He is also the international tax editor for www.property-tax-portal.co.uk.

James Bailey, Chartered Tax Advisor. James is an author and public speaker and provides valuable tax expertise to www.property-tax-portal.co.uk and www.taxinsider.co.uk.

Knowing Your Property Tax Strategy

1. Understanding your Tax Liabilities

Over the past few years property investment has become a very profitable way to make money.

Unfortunately there are very few people who consider the tax implications of their investment strategy before they decide to invest. Instead they take a view that they will address the tax issues when they decide to dispose of the property. This can be a very costly mistake as some simple planning can help to avoid large tax bills in the future.

The table below gives an indication of the tax that may be due if you follow any of the popular strategies outlined below.

Strategy	**Description**	**Income Tax**	**Capital Gains Tax**
Buy-to-let	Probably the most popular investment method and a strategy for long-term investment. Income tax will be due on the annual rental profits and CGT due when the property is disposed of.	Yes	Yes
Develop & Sell	This is typically classed as a short-term (i.e. 3-6 months) investment and only Income Tax is due if you are trading in properties in this way. All property development related expenditures can be offset against the final selling price.	Yes	No
Develop & Rent	Another typical long-term investment, where the property is developed and then rented out. All expenditures made developing the property can be offset when the property is disposed. However rental profit will be subject to annual income tax.	Yes	Yes

Buy & Sell	If your are a master or want to become a master of buying undervalued property and then re-selling at a higher price then you will be classed as a property trader and will typically be subject to Income Tax only.	Yes	No
Buy-let-live	A good investment strategy to make use of some very significant tax breaks if you are sitting on large capital gains. This strategy only really applies to investors who intent to hold only a small number of properties during their life-time i.e. (3-6 properties). Again income tax will be due on rental profits and CGT when the property is disposed of.	Yes	Yes (but is dramatically reduced)
Buy-live-let	Probably the most tax efficient way to avoid capital gains tax for the small investor. This increasingly popular strategy involves letting your previous main residence when buying a new home or moving abroad. Again income tax will be due on rental profits and CGT when the property is disposed of.	Yes	Yes (but is dramatically reduced)
Rent-a-Room	If you decide to rent-a-room that is part of your main residence then you can receive an annual rental income, to the value of £4,250 and not have any income tax liability. Ay income above this amount will be subject to income tax. CGT is not due if you sell your main residence which has been classed as your only home during the whole period of ownership.	Yes (if claiming rent-a-room relief and income is greater than £4,250)	No (if tenants live with the family owning the property)

	Please Note: if the tenants renting do not live together with the family, then there can be CGT on that part of the house rented out. See section 14 for more details		
Furnished Holiday Lets	If you let a furnished property as a holiday let, then you will be subject to income tax on any rental profits. There are number of very generous tax breaks available for those investing in Furnished Holiday Lets. See section 15 for more details	Yes	Yes

How to Slash your Property Income Tax

Before we look at the different income tax saving strategies, it is important to understand what is meant by the term **income tax** and when property investors and landlords are liable to pay it.

2. Income Tax Liabilities for Investors/Traders

Anybody investing in property is liable to pay income tax on any profitable income that is generated from their properties.

There are two main categories of people who invest in property, and both are liable to pay income tax. The characteristics of each are detailed in the following sections.

2.1. Property investor

If you invest in property for the long term, i.e., you have buy-to-let properties, then you will be referred to as a **property investor**. This is because you are holding on to a property for the long term.

If you are letting your investment properties, then you will be liable to pay income tax annually on the rental profits.

It is also likely that you will have another source of income, unless you have a large portfolio of properties where the rental income funds your lifestyle.

2.2. Property traders/dealers

If you are investing in property for the short term, i.e., 6–12 months, and intend to sell with the aim of generating a dealing profit, then you will be referred to as **property dealer** or **property trader**.

Property dealers and traders are liable to pay income tax when they sell the property.

You will find that most full-time property developers or renovators are classed as property dealers/traders.

2.3. Income Tax Rates

You can use the following link to view the income tax rates for previous years:

http://www.hmrc.gov.uk/rates/it.htm

The current rates of income tax for the 2006–2007 tax year are detailed in the table below:

INCOME TAX 2006–2007			
Rate/Allowance	***Rate***	***Band***	***Description***
Single-Person Allowance	Nil	£0 to £5,035	The first £5,035 of each individual's income is Tax Free.
Starting Rate	10%	£5,036 to £7,185	The next £2,150 is taxed at 10%. This means that any income between £5,036 and £7,185 will be taxed at this rate.
Basic Rate	22%	£7,186 to £38,335	The next £31,150 is taxed at 22%. This means that any income between £7,186 and £38,335 will be taxed at this rate.
Higher Rate	40%	> £38,335	Any income received above £38,335 will be taxed at 40%.

2.4. Income Tax Calculation Case Studies

Here are some case studies to illustrate how the tax liability is calculated for property investors and property dealers/traders.

2.4.1. Income tax calculation for property investors

The case study below illustrates the income tax liability for a basic-rate taxpayer.

Case Study - 1 : Income Tax Calculation for Property Investor (1)

John works as a local government officer and receives an annual salary of £20,000. He buys a property close to his local hospital for £45,000. He receives a monthly rental income of £400.

The property is let for the whole 2006–2007 tax year, which means that he has received an annual rental income of £4,800.

In the tax year he has also incurred property-related expenses of £2,000. These expenditures are made up as follows:

Expense	Amount
Interest repaid on mortgage	£1,200

Plumbing (to fix water leak)	£150
Annual gas safety inspection	£100
Central heating maintenance contract	£300
Replacement door fitted	£250
Total Expenditure	£2,000

This means that John's taxable rental profit is £2,800 (i.e., £4,800 – £2,000).

On this amount he is liable to pay tax at 22%. This is because he is a basic-rate taxpayer as his £20,000 salary falls into the basic tax rate band.

This means that he will pay tax at 22% on the rental profit of £2,800.

Therefore his tax liability is **£616** on the £2,800 profit.

The following case study illustrates how the rental income from the property pushes John into the higher-rate tax band.

Case Study - 2 : Income Tax Calculation for Property Investor (2)

This is the same scenario as in the previous case study. The only difference is that John has an annual salary of £36,000.

John's tax liability on the £2,800 profit is now calculated as follows.

The first £2,335 is taxed at the basic rate of 22%.

The remaining £465 is taxed at the higher rate of 40%. This is because the rental profit has taken his total income into the higher-rate tax band.

Therefore his tax liability is as follows:

(£2,335 × 0.22)	+	(£465 × 0.4)
£513.70	+	£186
	=	£699.70

John's tax liability is **£699.70** on the £2,800 profit.

2.4.2. *Income tax calculation for property developers*

The following case study illustrates how the income tax liability is calculated for a full-time property dealer.

Case Study - 3 : Income Tax Calculation for Property Dealer (1)

Bill works as a local government officer and earns a salary of £25,000. Bill prefers to become a property dealer, so he buys a run-down property for £50,000 in May 2005.

He spends £20,000 renovating and re-decorating the property before selling it six months later for £90,000.

This gives him a taxable profit of £20,000 (i.e., selling price – (purchase price + costs incurred on the property)).

Bill's tax liability on the £20,000 profit is made in the 2006–2007 tax year, so his tax liability is calculated as follows.

The first £13,335 is taxed at the basic rate of 22%.

The remaining £6,665 is taxed at the higher rate of 40%. This is because the rental profit has taken his total income into the higher-rate tax band.

Therefore his tax liability is as follows:

(£13,335 × 0.22) + (£6,665 × 0.4)
£2933.70 + £2,666

= £5,599.70

Bill's tax liability is **£5,599.70** n the £20,000 profit.

The following case study illustrates how the income tax liability is calculated for a part-time property dealer.

Case Study - 4 : Income Tax Calculation for Property Dealer (2)

Robert, a colleague of Bill and John, resigns from his job in the local government and decides to become a full-time property investor.

In his first year of dealing he buys two properties, renovates them, and sells them for a profit of £20,000 each. This means that he has a taxable income of £40,000. The profit is made in the 2006–2007 tax year, so his tax liability is calculated as follows.

- The first £5,035 is tax-free due to the personal allowance.
- The next £2,150 is taxed at the starting rate of 10%.

- The next £31,150 is taxed at the basic rate of £22%.
- The remaining £1,665 is taxed at the higher rate of 40%.

Here is the tax calculation:

Tax Rate	Amount	Tax Liability
Nil	£5,035	£0
10%	£2,150	£215
22%	£31,150	£6,853
40%	£1,665	£666
	Total Tax Liability	***£7,734***

Therefore Robert has a tax liability of ***£7,734*** on the £40,000 profit[1].

[1]Please note that if someone becomes a property dealer, this is a new self-employed trade, and they are liable for Class 4 National Insurance (NI) on the profits as well as for Class 2 NI; they must also inform the Revenue within three months of starting their new business.

3. Owning Properties as a Sole Trader

Holding a property in a sole name can be tax beneficial under certain circumstances.

In this section we will get to grips with why people hold properties as a sole trader and will learn about some of the tax benefits and drawbacks of owning properties in this way.

3.1. Buying Properties as a Sole Trader

A **sole trader** is an individual who buys properties in his or her sole name.

Although it is still a very common way to purchase properties, it is not necessarily the most tax efficient.

In most cases, properties are usually purchased as a sole trader for non-tax-related reasons.

Here are the two most common non-tax-related reasons why you might decide to buy property as a sole trader.

a) You don't have a partner who you can invest with.

b) You don't want to invest with anybody else; that is, you can't trust anybody, or you want total control over your investment.

If you have invested for either of these reasons, then you can still make tax savings.

3.2. When is it Tax Efficient to Buy Property as a Sole Trader?

The ideal scenario for buying a property as a sole trader is if you have no income.

The reason for this is because you can utilise your annual, tax-free personal allowance.

In simple terms, the farther your income is from the higher-rate tax band, the more you will save in income tax by having the property in your sole name. This is especially true if your partner is a higher-rate taxpayer.

The following two case studies illustrate these points.

Case Study - 5 : Sole Trader With No Income

Joanne is a married woman but does not work. Her husband is a high-flying executive who earns £70,000 per annum.

Upon the death of a relative, Joanne is left £100,000. She uses the entirety of this inheritance to purchase an investment property.

She makes £380 rental profit per month. (Her expenditures are low as she bought the property with cash, so therefore she has no outstanding mortgage.)

This means that she makes an annual rental profit of £4,560.

She is not liable to pay any tax on this amount as it is within the annual personal income tax allowance of £5,035.

Had Joanne bought the property in joint ownership with her husband, then he would have been liable to pay tax at 40% on his share of the investment. If his share of the property was 50%, then he would have an annual tax liability of £912.

This means that over a 10-year period, Joanne will see a minimum tax savings of £9,120 by owning the property in her sole name.

Case Study - 6 : Property Investor With No Income, but Partner Works

Lisa is a married woman and earns £15,000 per annum as a store sales assistant. Her husband is a hotel manager and earns £45,000 per annum.

They decide that they want to start investing in property and purchase a property for £45,000.

They take tax advice before investing and are told that they will pay less annual income tax if the property is purchased in Lisa's sole name.

This is because she is not a higher-rate taxpayer.

3.3. When is it NOT Tax Efficient to Buy Property as a Sole Trader?

Try not to buy property as a sole trader if you are a higher-rate taxpayer, especially if you can invest with a partner who is a lower-rate taxpayer.

If you are a higher-rate taxpayer, then you will have to pay income tax on any rental income at the higher rate as well.

It would be very poor tax planning on your end if you ended up paying 40% tax on all rental income, especially if you had a partner who was a lower-rate taxpayer.

3.4. How Do I Get a Mortgage If I Have No Income?

This is a very commonly asked question, especially by those families in which one partner does not work.

After all, if the other partner is a taxpayer (especially a higher-rate one), then it makes sense to buy investment property in the name of the non-working partner. This is to make use of their annual personal allowance.

In today's flexible mortgage market you can get a mortgage if you have little or even no income at all. However, you will probably have to pay a higher rate of interest and will have fewer lenders to choose from.

The banks may well ask for a guarantor just in case you fail to make mortgage repayments.

So, if you either inherit or are given a lump sum of money and you can find somebody who has faith in your property investment ideas—who is willing to act as a guarantor—then you can invest in the property market and start making use of that annual tax-free personal allowance!

There is no shortage of mortgage lending companies and Web sites where you can browse the products that are available.

You might find the following two sites particularly useful:

http://www.moneyextra.com;
http://www.paragon-mortgages.co.uk.

PLEASE NOTE: As with any financial decision, it is important that you speak to a regulated financial advisor before deciding on a particular product.

3.5. A Note About Selling Properties When Operating as a Sole Trader

You now know when it is beneficial to buy properties as a sole trader.

However, it is generally better to have a property in a joint name when you come to sell the property. The main exception to this rule is if the property has been your PPR; see section 17 for further details.

4. Income Tax & Property Partnerships

There is no doubt that owning properties in a partnership can be an excellent income tax–saving strategy.

In this section you will learn how owning properties in partnerships can significantly reduce your income tax bill.

4.1. What is a Property Partnership?

To put it simply, a property partnership exists when two or more people own a property in joint names.

When a property is held as a partnership, it is usually held in either of the following two ways.

4.1.1. Joint tenants

This method is most commonly used when a husband and wife purchase a property together.

The most important point about this method of ownership is that when one of the joint tenants dies, the surviving tenant becomes the sole owner.

Case Study - 7 : Owning Properties as Joint Tenants

Lisa and Alex are husband and wife and own a property as joint tenants. Unfortunately, Lisa passes away due to ill health.

The property now becomes the sole ownership of Alex.

4.1.2. Tenants in common

This method is used when the owners of the property want to register the fact that they have separate ownership. This method is most commonly used when two or more unconnected people purchase a property together.

The most important point to note about this method is that when one of the 'tenants in common' dies, the property does not necessarily become the ownership of the surviving tenants.

Case Study - 8 : Owning Properties as 'Tenants in Common'

Jack and Bill are two long-term friends who decide to start investing in properties together.

They are also both married.

Jack is the wealthier of the two, so when they decide to purchase a property, he funds 60% of the deposit. Therefore it is agreed that the property will be a 60:40 split in Jack's favour.

They purchase the property as 'tenants in common,' where they specify that the property will be passed to their estate should either party die.

Jack is the first to pass away. Upon his death, his 60% ownership in the property is passed to his wife.

4.2. When to Consider Buying in a Partnership

As we saw in section 3, you should generally try to avoid owning a property as a sole trader if you are a higher-rate taxpayer. This is purely because you will be liable to pay tax at the higher rate on any profitable rental income.

The two most important conditions that must be satisfied before investing with a partner are that

a) your partner must be a lower rate taxpayer than yourself; that is, if you pay tax at 40%, then your partner should pay tax at 22% or less;

b) you MUST be able to trust your partner(s).

Let's look at both these points in more detail in the following sections.

4.3. Having a Partner who is a Lower-Rate Taxpayer

The table below shows when you *will* and when you *will not* have income tax savings by investing with a partner.

Tax Rate	Partners Tax Rate	Tax Saving?	Comment
40%	Nil	Yes	Having a partnership with a nil-rate partner will give you the <u>GREATEST</u> tax savings.
40%	10%	Yes	Your partner will get taxed at up to 30% less than you!
40%	22%	Yes	Still considerable tax savings to be had.
40%	40%	No	You both pay tax at the same rate.
22%	Nil	Yes	Again, you will have tax savings as your partner is a zero-rate taxpayer.
22%	10%	Yes	You partner will pay up to 12% less tax than you.
22%	22%	No	You both pay tax at the same rate.
22%	40%	No	No tax saving here as your partner will be taxed at a higher rate than you.
10%	Nil	Yes	Even though the 10% tax band is such a small band, you will still have tax savings.
10%	10%	No	You both pay tax at the same rate.
10%	22%	No	No tax savings here as your partner will be taxed at a higher rate than you.
10%	40%	No	No tax savings here as your partner will be taxed at a higher rate than you.
Nil	Nil	No	You both pay tax at the same rate.
Nil	10%	No	No tax savings here as your partner will be taxed at a higher rate than you.
Nil	22%	No	No tax savings here as your partner will be taxed at a higher rate than you.
Nil	40%	No	No tax savings here as your partner will be taxed at a higher rate than you.

As you can see from the table, the amount of tax you will save depends on the tax bands in which you and your partner(s) lie.

To summarise:

The biggest income tax savings occur when you pay tax at 40% and your partner is a nil-rate taxpayer. In this scenario, it really does make sense to have a partnership.

This is because you will be passing on a portion of the rental profit to your partner, who will be able to use his/her annual income tax personal allowance.

Case Study - 9 : Income Tax Savings Using a Partnership

Jack is a bachelor and earns £50,000 in a well-paid city job. He meets Joanne, the girl of his dreams, and eventually, they both decide to get married.

Joanne gives up work shortly after the marriage.

They can no longer live in Jack's one-bedroom city apartment, so they buy a new house, and at the same time they decide to rent out the existing apartment.

Jack moves the apartment into joint ownership with his wife.

The annual rental profit on the apartment is £4,000 per annum. This means that each is liable to pay tax on £2,000.

Joanne has no tax liability as her £2,000 profit is consumed by her personal tax allowance, whereas Jack has an £800 tax liability on his share of the profits.

This means that by transferring the property, they will have an annual tax savings of £800 per annum.

Over a 10-year period, this is a tax savings of £8,000!

PLEASE NOTE: An even greater tax savings could be had if Jack transferred the entire property into his wife's name. However, Jack does not want to lose ownership rights on a property that was originally his. Therefore he only transfers half of the ownership to his wife.

Tax Tip - 1

If you are already a nil-rate taxpayer, then don't go looking for a partner who is a higher-rate taxpayer.

This is because you will be unnecessarily passing on an income tax liability to your partner.

Instead, consider keeping the property in your sole name until your rental profits lead you to incur a tax liability at a rate that is equal to or greater than that of your partner.

4.4. Partners Must Be TRUSTWORTHY

If you buy property in a partnership, then you MUST make sure that the partners with whom you are purchasing are people who you **implicitly** trust, e.g., a spouse, your mother, your father, etc.

This is not just for tax reasons; it is simply good **BUSINESS PRACTICE**.

4.5. Partnerships Between Husband and Wife

> **Tax Tip - 2**
> The Inland Revenue will treat all properties purchased between husband and wife (other than shares in a close company) as a 50:50 split, unless otherwise stated.

In fact, the Inland Revenue treats all jointly owned property between husband and wife as an equal 50:50 split, unless otherwise stated.

This means that unless you tell the Inland Revenue otherwise, you will both be taxed 50:50 on any property rental profits.

A considerable amount of tax can be saved by having a property jointly owned by husband and wife, especially if one or the other is a nil- or a lower-rate taxpayer. It is important to note that if you intend to have a property between husband and wife as a non-50:50 split, then you must have an agreement between the two of you to say that this is the case.

It is not enough to just make a declaration to the Inland Revenue stating that a property is owned in unequal shares. It must actually be owned in this manner, and documentary evidence must be made available if requested by the Inland Revenue.

The following case study illustrates this scenario along with considerable tax savings.

Case Study - 10 : Potential Tax Savings Between Husband and Wife

After five years of marital bliss, John and Lisa decide to buy an investment property.

John is a higher-rate taxpayer, whereas Lisa is a homemaker and therefore has no income.

They buy a two-bedroom terraced house for £80,000. They decide to have the property as a 90:10 split between the two of them in favour of Lisa and produce documentary evidence to support this. They also inform the Inland Revenue of this split.

(The property is split in this manner to take advantage of Lisa's personal income tax allowance—in other words, they want to reduce their tax bill!)

They make £4,000 rental profit on the property on an annual basis. This means that the profit is split as follows:

- Lisa's share of the profit is £3,600;
- John's share of the profit is £400.

Lisa has no tax liability as her profit is within her tax allowance, and John pays £160 tax his £400 profit.

If the property had remained as a 50:50 split, then the total joint tax liability would have been £800.

Therefore they have an annual savings of £640! Over 10 years, this gives tax savings of at least £6,400.

4.6. Partnerships Between Those Other Than a Husband and Wife

Tax Tip - 3

If a property is purchased as a partnership between those other than a husband and wife, you **MUST** inform the Inland Revenue of the split.

In this type of partnership the Inland Revenue does not make any assumptions as to how the property is split. It is the taxpayer's duty to tell the Inland Revenue how the property has been split, and it must be based on fact.

For example, if you buy a property in a partnership with a friend, in which he or she provides 70% of the deposit and you provide 30% of the deposit, then you must also inform the Inland Revenue of the 70:30 split.

4.7. How to Declare a Partnership Split to the Inland Revenue

If you are a husband and wife wanting an unequal split, then you must make a declaration to the Inland Revenue about the ownership split.

Such a declaration takes effect from the date it is made, providing notice of the declaration is given to the Inland Revenue via Form 17 within 60 days.

If you would like to download a copy of Form 17, please visit the following link:

http://www.hmrc.gov.uk/pdfs/form17.pdf

It is important to note that the form only covers the assets listed on it. This means that if you have other properties, they must also be listed to make the Inland Revenue aware of split.

Evidence of the ownership of the asset should also be provided to the Revenue together with Form 17.

Please note that different Revenue offices differ with regards to what evidence is required to prove the ownership split for a property.

There are two common ways to prove the split.

a) Provide a signed declaration by the two parties concerned detailing that ownership of the joint property is split in a specific way.

This is acceptable to some Revenue officers.

However, other officers will want more formal proof.

b) Provide more formal property documents that include the following:
   i. the deeds of conveyance;
   ii. bank accounts (to see letters to and from the bank confirming the change).

The best thing is just to send in (a), but be prepared to send in (b) if the Revenue requires it or asks any further questions.

4.8. Moving Properties Into Joint Ownership to Avoid Income Tax

If you have realised from this strategy that you can save tax by holding your property in a partnership, then you may well be thinking about how to transfer to joint ownership.

Well, it is actually very easy to do, and you will incur *no* capital gains tax liability if you are transferring part ownership to your spouse, i.e., your husband or wife.

PLEASE NOTE: If part ownership of the property is to be transferred to anybody other than your spouse, then there may be a capital gains tax liability triggered.

4.8.1. Three simple steps to follow for moving into joint ownership

The following three steps will show you how you can transfer the property into joint ownership.

STEP 1. Contact your mortgage lender.

Tell your mortgage lender that you want to transfer the property into joint ownership, and explain why you want to do this.

Your mortgage lender will then send you a new mortgage application form for you to complete in order to move the property into joint ownership.

Unfortunately, lenders will treat transferring an existing property into joint ownership as though you are applying for a new mortgage. Therefore it is very likely that you will have to submit the same paperwork again and effectively apply for a new mortgage.

It is likely that the property will be put into joint names on the same terms as the original contract; that is, if the original mortgage was fixed at 4.99% and had four years left to run on the fixed period, then the new mortgage will also be the same.

However, if mortgage rates have reduced, then be cheeky and ask if you can also have it at the new reduced interest rate!

STEP 2. Contact a solicitor.

Once your mortgage application has been approved, your solicitor can have all relevant documents changed into joint names pretty quickly. It usually takes about four weeks to complete all the legal paperwork.

Also, tell your solicitor whether you want the property to be owned as 'Joint tenants' or as 'Tenants in common', and how you want to split the ownership of the property. For example you may want to hold the property in the majority of the lower rate tax payer, so that you pay less tax.

Whenever a property is being purchased by more than one person or transferred into multiple ownership you solicitor should always ask you how you wish to hold the property.

STEP 3. Notify the Inland Revenue.

If you decide to have an unequal ownership split, then tell the Inland Revenue of this split as soon as possible.

Don't delay in notifying the Inland Revenue as it could well cost you in tax penalties.

4.8.2. Typical costs incurred when transferring

The costs that you are likely to incur when transferring the property will include the following:

- **Solicitor costs:** These are normally between £300 and £400. However, they will be less than the amount charged when buying a new house as searches will not need to be carried out again.

- **Mortgage lender fees:** The mortgage lender may or may not charge a fee for re-issuing the mortgage in joint names.

- **Stamp duty:** This may be payable dependant upon the mortgage amount that is being transferred. For example, if you are transferring £125,000 of the mortgage amount to your partner, then stamp duty will be payable at the rate of 1%; that is, £1,250 in stamp duty will be payable.

- **A valuation fee may also be incurred, especially if you are using the mortgage re-application** as an opportunity to release some equity from the property.

Please see section 13 to learn more about stamp duty.

It is important that you consider the tax savings you will make before you decide to transfer a property into joint names.

Ideally, you should calculate the cost of transferring the property into joint names and then consider how much income tax you will save on an annual basis.

The case study below demonstrates the importance of making such considerations.

Case Study - 11 : Saving Tax When Moving a Property Into Joint Ownership

Alex has an investment property in his sole name and is a higher-rate taxpayer.

His wife, Lisa, is unemployed and has no intention of working.

Alex has an outstanding mortgage of £50,000 on the property, which is now worth £100,000.

He gifts 75% of the property to his wife and re-mortgages the property in joint names, with a 75:25 split in favour of his wife.

The cost of re-mortgaging is as follows:

- Solicitor costs	£300
- Mortgage lender fees	£150
- Stamp duty	N/A. This is because 75% of the £50,000 mortgage is £37,500, and this amount is below the stamp duty threshold value.

He also calculates what the tax savings will be on an annual basis on a property income of £6,000.

Alex's tax liability	➔ 40% on £1,500 = £600	(based on 25% ownership)
Lisa's tax liability	➔ 0% on £4,500 = £0	(based on 75% ownership)

By having a 75:25 split, the combined tax liability is £600.

If Alex had kept the property in his sole ownership, then his tax liability would have been £2,400 (40% on £6,000 taxable property income) on an annual basis.

This means that both Alex and Lisa are making an annual income tax savings of £1,800.

As you can see, the cost incurred in transferring the property is not even a third of the tax savings they get in the first year alone!

5. Offsetting Interest Charges

In this section you will learn about the different types of interest repayments that property investors may come across.

More importantly, you will understand when each of these types of interest can and cannot be offset against your rental income.

5.1. Interest on Mortgages

It is probably fair to say that this is the most common type of interest that is associated with property investors.

This interest relates to the amount you pay back to your mortgage lender that is above and beyond the initial amount that you borrowed.

> **Tax Tip - 4**
> It does not matter if the mortgage is a 'repayment' or an 'interest only' mortgage. The fact that interest repayments have been made means that they can be offset.

This is illustrated through the following case study.

> **Case Study - 12 : Interest on Mortgages**
>
> John buys an investment property for £100,000.
>
> The finance for the property is made up from a £20,000 deposit (provided from his personal savings) and an £80,000 buy-to-let mortgage (provided by a High Street Bank).
>
> In the first year of the mortgage he pays £2,500 in mortgage interest. This entire amount can be offset against his income from the property.
>
> This means that if he received £5,500 income from his property, he would only be liable to pay tax on £3,000.

5.2. A note about 'interest only' and 'repayment mortgages'

As mentioned in the above tax tip, you are able to claim interest relief regardless of whether you have an 'interest only' mortgage or a 'repayment' mortgage.

5.2.1. Interest Only Mortgage

With an **interest only** mortgage you do actually only pay the interest that is charged on the amount that has been borrowed. The actual amount i.e. the capital amount remains the same and is usually due in one lump sum at the end of the mortgage term.

Case Study - 13 : Interest only mortgage

Louise buys a property for £125,000 where her mortgage lender provides £100,000 on an interest only mortgage over 25 years.

Her monthly interest repayment is £500. She is able to offset the entire amount against the rental income.

However at the end of the mortgage term, she will still owe the £100,000 that has been borrowed.

5.2.2. Repayment Mortgage

With a **repayment** mortgage you pay both the interest and the capital amount on a monthly basis. However you are only able to offset the amount that has been charged in interest. You cannot offset the capital repayments.

Case Study - 14 : Repayment mortgage

Same scenario as in the previous example. However this time Louise goes for a repayment mortgage of £100,000.

This means that her monthly repayments will be higher because she is repaying both the interest and part of the capital amount borrowed.

She makes monthly repayments of £650, where £400 is the interest repayment and £250 is capital repayment.

She is only able to offset the interest part of the repayment i.e. the £400. She is not able to offset the capital element of the repayment mortgage.

5.3. Interest on Personal Loans

Tax Tip - 5

If you take out a personal loan that is used 'wholly and exclusively' for the purpose of the property, then the interest charged on this loan can also be offset.

The important point to note here is that personal loans *must* be used in connection with the property.

Following are some typical property investment scenarios detailing when the interest charged on a personal loan *can* be offset against the property income.

5.3.1. Loan used for providing deposit

Most buy-to-let mortgage lenders require you to provide a 20% deposit before they will lend you the remaining 80% in the form of a mortgage.

If you don't have the 20% deposit, then it is likely that you may well need to finance the deposit by getting a personal loan.

If you do take out a personal loan for the 20% deposit, the interest charged on this loan can be offset against the property income.

If you are considering doing this, or have already done this, then what this means is that you have a 100% financed investment property, where interest charged on both the mortgage and the personal loan can be offset against the rental income.

Case Study - 15 : Interest on personal loan used for deposit

Ali is desperate to buy his first investment property after seeing his pension fund plummet and his house value almost double within 5 years.

Unfortunately, (due to his lavish lifestyle), he has no savings of his own but is in a well paid job, earning £40,000 per annum.

He sees an investment property advertised for £100,000, but his mortgage lender requests a deposit of £15,000.

He sources this deposit by acquiring a personal loan at a rate of 9% per annum.

The bank then agrees to finance the remaining £85,000.

This means that Ali has a 100% financed investment property. Therefore he is able to offset the interest charged on both his loan and the BTL mortgage against his rental income.

5.3.2. Loan used for refurbishments/developments

Periodically, you will need to refurbish or even develop a property.

Imagine that you have just purchased a property that needs totally re-decorating and modernising. If you take out a loan for this kind of work, then the interest charged on the loan can be offset against the property income.

Alternatively, you might decide to embark on a more expensive property extension, e.g., to build a conservatory.

Again, the same rule applies here: The interest charged on the loan can be offset.

Case Study - 16 : Interest on personal loan used for a refurbishment

Karen buys an investment property for £100,000. She manages to pay the 15% deposit from her own personal savings and the remaining finance is acquired on a BTL mortgage.

Before letting out the property she decides that a new bathroom suite will greatly increase the chances of the property getting let quickly. She prices a replacement bathroom suite at £2,000.

Unfortunately she has already stretched her personal savings account by funding the deposit for the property.

Therefore she applies for, and is successful, in obtaining a £2,000 personal loan at an interest rate of 10%.

Because the personal loan is used to replace the bathroom suite in the investment property she is able to offset the entire interest charged on the loan against her rental income.

5.3.3. Loans used for purchasing products

If you purchase goods from retailers where finance is available and these goods are used in your property, then the interest charged can also be offset.

This is more likely to happen if you are providing a fully furnished property, e.g., a luxury apartment.

If this is the case, then you may decide to buy the more expensive items on finance.

Such items are likely to include

- sofas, dining table & chairs, beds;
- cooker, washing machine, fridge/freezer;
- carpets, flooring, etc.

If you are paying for these products over a period of time (e.g., 6, 12, or 18 months), then any interest charged by your creditor can be offset against your rental income.

Case Study - 17 : Interest on buy-now-pay-later loans

Continuing from the previous case study.

Once the bathroom suite has been replaced she decides that the property should be offered fully furnished.

She decides to buy some new kitchen furniture in a sale and buys it on a buy-now-pay later scheme where interest is charged at a rate of 27.9%.

Again she is able to offset the interest charged on the loan against the rental income.

5.3.4. Loans to continue the running of your business

There may be occasions when you need to borrow money because your need to pay some bills or employees but do not have sufficient funds in your account.

In such circumstances you may decide to apply for a short-term loan to make these payments. Again the interest charged on the loan can be offset against the property income.

Case Study - 18 : Interest on loan for paying bills & employees

Alexander has a large portfolio of properties but has incurred a cash flow problem. This is because he has just paid for a major refurbishment on one of his properties by using funds in his property account, rather than acquiring some sort of finance.

This decision means that he is unable to pay his employees (who work in his property business) their end of month salaries and some property related utility bills that are due.

He applies for a short-term loan of £5,000 to make the necessary payments and interest is charged at 8%.

His is able to offset the interest charged against the income from his properties because it is incurred for the purpose of his property business.

5.3.5. Interest on overdrafts

If you have a separate bank account set-up for your property investment business then you may decide to apply for an overdraft rather than a personal loan.

If you decide to do this then as long as the overdraft is used for the purpose of the property business then you can offset the interest charged on the overdraft.

Case Study - 19 : Interest charged on overdrafts

Using the previous example.

Instead of applying for a loan, Alexander decides to request a one-year overdraft limit on his account of £5,000. His application is successful and he is charged an interest rate of 7.5%.

Whenever he uses his overdraft facility and interest is charged, he is able to offset it against his rental income.

5.4. When You Cannot Offset the Interest Charged on Personal Loans

You now have a good understanding of when interest charged on loans can be offset against the property rental income.

Now consider the following:

a) loans used for paying for a family holiday;
b) loans used for buying a new car;
c) loans used for paying children's tuition fees, etc.

It is clear from the above examples that all these scenarios have one common characteristic:

They have ABSOLUTELY NOTHING to do with the property investment!

So, it is suffice to say that if the loan has nothing to do with your property investment, then any interest repayments cannot be offset.

To help you decide if an interest repayment on a loan can be offset, always ask yourself the following: 'Is the loan being used for the sole purpose of my property?'

If the answer is **YES**, then you can generally offset the interest.

If the answer is **NO**, then you cannot offset the interest.

5.5. Interest on Re-mortgages

If you have a mortgage on your investment property, then it is highly likely that you will consider moving to another lender at some point.

The main reason for this is because you will be trying hard to find a better mortgage deal!

As interest rates have been falling over the past few years, more and more people have been re-mortgaging their investment properties to capitalise on the better deals and to help grow their property portfolios.

Below are some pointers about re-mortgaging.

a) If you re-mortgage your outstanding mortgage with another lender, then you can *still* offset the interest repayments.

Case Study - 20 : Interest on Re-mortgages

Timothy has an outstanding mortgage balance of £50,000 on his investment property. He decides to move his mortgage from the Nat West to LloydsTSB as they are offering a lower rate of interest.

Timothy can still offset the entire interest charged by LloydsTSB on the £50,000 re-mortgage.

b) If you re-mortgage for a lower amount, then you can still offset the whole mortgage interest.

Case Study - 21 : Re-mortgaging for a Different Value

Imagine the same scenario as in the previous example, where Timothy has an outstanding balance of £50,000 on his investment mortgage.

However, he inherits £20,000 from a family member, so he decides to use this toward lowering his mortgage liability.

Therefore he only re-mortgages to the value of £30,000 with LloydsTSB.

Again, the entire interest charged on the £30,000 can be offset against the property income.

c) If you re-mortgage for a greater amount, then generally speaking you can only offset the additional amount if it is used for the purpose of an investment property (however you may be able to exploit paragraph 45700 (see Understanding paragraph 45700).

As property prices have sharply risen over the past few years, investors have been re-mortgaging their properties for higher values.

This is known as **releasing equity.**

If you have released equity or are considering doing this, then you need to follow the guidelines given above regarding the interest charged on personal loans.

You need to ask yourself,

'Is the additional equity release being used for the sole purpose of my property business?'

This can be illustrated through the following case study.

Case Study - 22 : Releasing Equity

Timothy has an outstanding balance of £50,000 on his investment mortgage.

However, his property value has appreciated considerably, so he decides to re-mortgage with LloydsTSB for £80,000.

This means that he is releasing additional equity out of his current property to the value of £30,000.

He decides to use the equity release in the following way:

£20,000 is used to fund a new property investment, and it provides the deposit for his next buy-to-let investment. £10,000 is used to pay for a new car for his wife.

Now, Timothy can *only* offset the interest charged on both the outstanding mortgage balance of £50,000 and the £20,000 he is using as a deposit for his next purchase.

This is because this combined amount of £70,000 is used 'wholly and exclusively' for his property investments.

However, he *cannot* use the interest charged on £10,000 for buying the car as this cost is not associated with his property investments.

d) Generally speaking, because it is possible to obtain a lower rate of interest on your residential mortgage, more and more investors are deciding to increase the borrowing on their main residence and using this to reduce the investment mortgages.

Case Study - 23 : Releasing Equity from main residence

Jack and Louise have a residential mortgage on their private residence for £100,000. The interest rate is fixed at 4.5%. They also have a BTL investment property. The outstanding mortgage on this property is also £100,000 but the interest rate is at a higher rate of 6.5%.

Because their main residence has a value of £300,000, they release £100,000 equity from their main residence, at the same rate of 4.5%, and pay off the outstanding debt of £100,000 on the investment property.

Again the interest charged on the £100,000 equity release can be offset against the rental income off the investment property.

5.6. Purchasing a Property With Cash and Then Re-mortgaging

Serious property investors are always looking for deals.

When one comes their way, it is sometimes not feasible to apply for finance. This is because the administration and paperwork will take too long, and this is likely to result in the investor losing out on the deal.

In such scenarios the investor will end up buying the property through their cash reserves, and they will then re-mortgage the property to release the invested funds.

The question then arises as to whether the interest charged on the re-mortgage is tax deductible.

In Arthur Weller's opinion, the mortgage interest is tax deductible in such scenarios. This is because the property was bought with the *intention* to take out the mortgage soon afterward.

In such scenarios the purchaser will only pay cash originally because this is a better way to execute the purchase.

Case Study - 24 : Cash Purchase and Then Re-mortgaging

John has inherited £100,000 from his father's estate.

He is presented with the opportunity to purchase a property at £100,000, but he must complete the purchase within two weeks. By purchasing within two weeks, he will save £25,000 off the original asking price of £125,000.

John knows that it will take too long to apply for a BTL mortgage, so he pays for the property in cash.

Two months later, he re-mortgages the property using a standard BTL mortgage.

In this scenario, John can offset the interest on the re-mortgage as it was always his *intention* to fund the investment by a mortgage.

5.7. Interest Paid When Using Credit Cards

There are a growing number of people who either buy products or borrow money on their credit cards. The credit cards are either used to finance purchases for their investment properties, or money is withdrawn to fund a deposit.

Tax Specialist Ian McTernan, gives the following guidance about the use of credit cards.

Credit Card Funding

Generally speaking, interest paid on credit cards is *not* a deductible expense.

The reasons for this are as follows.

1. It is difficult to determine which part of the outstanding balance relates to the property and which relates to general consumer spending.

2. The Revenue takes a dim view of borrowing on credit cards, in general, as the level of interest charged is above what they will accept as a 'normal commercial rate.'

3. The borrowing can be easily 'tainted' by using the card for other purposes.

4. It is near impossible to get a certificate of 'interest paid' from a credit card company. This means that it is extremely difficult to prove what portion of the interest is attributed to the property.

5. A more technical reason is that credit card interest does not fall into the definition of 'loan interest' or 'annual payments' as far as the Revenue is concerned.

Let's look at the following case study.

Case Study - 25 : Using Credit Cards

John borrows £5,000 on his credit card to use as a deposit for his buy-to-let property. He has an outstanding balance of £1,500. He normally spends £1,000 a month on his card and pays £1,200 per month.

Let's assume that an interest rate of 20% applies on any outstanding balance that is carried forward.

At the end of the month, John's balance before his payment is £7,500 and after his payment is £6,300. How much of the £5,000 has been paid off? Is it £Nil as the payment is set off against the previously outstanding balance, £1,200 if set against the borrowings, or some figure in between?

After a few months, it becomes impossible to define what interest relates to the borrowing and what relates to his normal activity on the card.

The test for any expense claimed as a deduction is 'wholly and exclusively,' and obviously, this test is not met, and hence no allowance is given.

Taking this one step further, it is possible to obtain a tax deduction where the credit card company offers a 'personal loan' account, whereby you write out a cheque for a purchase, and this appears in a completely separate account. This is because it is possible to satisfy the 'wholly and exclusively' test.

5.8. Understanding paragraph 45700

Although we have generally stated that it is not possible to offset interest on a loan if it is not used for the purpose of the property, there is a ruling which is mentioned paragraph 45700 of the Inland Revenue Business Income Manual.

This ruling has been highlighted by a number of tax specialists and when used it can produce significant benefits for landlords. In particular it was highlighted by Maurice Parry-Wingfield (Tax Director at Deloitte) in the 18th September 2004 edition of the Financial Times.

Paragraph 45700 gives landlords the opportunity to release equity from their investment properties and offset the interest regardless of what the equity release was used for.

The only restriction is that the equity release cannot be greater than the market value of the property when it is brought into the letting business. If the property had been originally bought for letting, this amount would be the purchase cost of the property.

In paragraph 45700, the Inland Revenue provides the following example:

'Mr A owns a flat in central London, which he bought ten years ago for £125,000. He has a mortgage of £80,000 on the property. He has been offered a job in Holland and is moving there to live and work. He intends to come back to the UK at some time. He decides to keep his flat and rent it out while he is away. His London flat now has a market value of £375,000. He renegotiates his mortgage on the flat to convert it to a buy to let mortgage and borrows a further £125,000. He withdraws the £125,000 which he then uses to buy a flat in Rotterdam.

The Inland Revenue goes on to say that 'Although he has withdrawn capital from the business the interest on the mortgage loan is allowable in full because it is **funding the transfer of the property to the business at its open market value** at the time the business started. The capital account is not overdrawn'.

Here are some more case studies to explain the benefits of this tax break for landlords and homeowners.

5.8.1. Benefiting from Interest Relief When Buying Off-Plan

Case Study - 26 : Benefiting from interest relief when buying off-plan

Alex buys an investment property off plan in January 2002 for £125,000. When the property is completed in June 2003 it is worth £175,000. Upon completion Alex decides to let the property and therefore the property is transferred to the lettings business at a value of £175,000.

This means that in the future years, Alex can remortgage the property for an additional £50,000 and still offset the interest that is charged. It does not matter what the £50,000 equity release is used for, it can be offset against the rental income, as the market value of the property at the time of letting was £175,000.

So if Alex wants to use the £50,000 equity to buy a new sports car then the interest charged on the equity release can be offset against the rental income.

It is important to understand that Alex is not allowed to offset any interest charges for equity that is released above £175,000 unless it is used for the purpose of the lettings business.

So this means that if in future years the property is valued at £300,000, then although he may be able to release additional equity above £175,000 he will not be able to offset interest on this amount if it used for anything other than the lettings business.

A tax efficient way to invest in property is to let out your existing residence and move into a new property (this is covered in further detail in section 18). This is because you will receive in particular two very generous tax saving reliefs:

- The '36 Month Rule' and
- Private Letting Relief

For more details about these rules, please go to section 18 18.

5.8.2. Benefiting from Interest Relief When Letting Out Your Own Home

Case Study - 27 : Benefiting from interest relief when letting out your own home

John and Louise buy a house in 1987 for £50,000. They live in it for 14 years and then decide to move to a bigger house. Instead of selling the existing house they decide to let it out.

Over the 14 years the house has been fully paid for and therefore there is no outstanding mortgage.
The value of the house in 2001 is £190,000. The new house that they have seen is £300,000.

In order to provide the deposit for the new house, they re-mortgage their existing house on a buy-to-let mortgage for £152,000. This amount is used to fund the deposit on the new residence, which means that they only need to borrow £148,000.

The entire interest that is charged on the buy-to-let mortgage can be offset against the rental income. This is because it is below the market value of the property at the time of letting.

Two years later the original property is worth £250,000. In order to reduce the mortgage on their private residence, they are able to release an additional £38,000 of equity on the buy-to-let mortgage. This means that they have mortgaged to the amount of £190,000 on this property.

Again, because they have not gone over the market value of the property at the time of letting they are able to offset the entire interest charges against the rental income.

At the same time they have also successfully managed to reduce the interest on their private residence by an additional £38,000!

Once again, if the original property is remortgaged above £190,000 and the money is not used for the purpose of the lettings business then the interest charged cannot be offset against the rental income.

6. 10% Wear and Tear or Renewals?

In this section you will learn about two very important methods that can be used to reduce your income tax bill.

These two methods are known as:

- the **10% Wear and Tear Allowance** and
- the **renewals basis** method.

They are relatively simple strategies to understand, and they both relate to the furnishings provided in a property.

However, so many investors get confused by not knowing which method they can use and how it will affect their annual property income tax bill.

Choosing the right one can have a significant bearing on your income tax liability.

6.1. What is the 10% Wear and Tear Allowance?

The 10% Wear and Tear Allowance is an allowance that the Inland Revenue has introduced to make the lives of property investors easier when they complete their tax returns.

In a nutshell, it allows you to offset 10% of your annual rental income against your property income tax bill.

This sounds straightforward, and in principle, it is. However, there are some important points to note.

a) The Inland Revenue states that

   'The Wear and Tear Allowance is calculated by taking 10 percent of the next rental received for the furnished residential accommodation. To find the 'net rent' you deduct charges and services that would normally be borne by a tenant but are, in fact, borne by you (for example, council tax, water and sewerage rates etc.).'

   In most cases, it is very straightforward to calculate.

b) It does not matter how much you, as a landlord, spend on furnishing your property. You can only offset 10% of your net rental income.

c) If you use this allowance, then the Inland Revenue states that:

   'it isn't possible to chop and change between the wear and tear allowance and the renewals allowance from year to year'.

d) The allowance can be used from the day that your property becomes furnished.

6.2. Understanding When the Allowance Can Be Used

> **Tax Tip - 6**
> The 10% Wear and Tear Allowance can *only* be claimed when a property is **fully furnished.**

Before we go any further, it is worthwhile understanding what is meant by a **fully furnished** property.

Here is the Inland Revenue's definition:

'A furnished property is one which is capable of normal occupation without the tenant having to provide their own beds, chairs, tables, sofas and other furnishings, cooker, etc.'

What this means is that a tenant can start living out of the property as soon as they move in. The only accessories that the tenant needs to provide are his/her own personal belongings.

More importantly, this means that the 10% Wear and Tear Allowance cannot be used for partly furnished or un-furnished properties.

Here are a couple of case studies to illustrate the use of this rule.

Case Study - 28 : Simple Calculation of Wear and Tear Allowance

John rents out a fully furnished property.

He receives a monthly rent of £500.

The tenant is responsible for all property bills (i.e., utility bills) and services provided to the property (e.g., gardening).

The annual income for the property is therefore £6,000.

This means that John can offset £600 when he calculates his rental profits.

Case Study - 29 : Complex Calculation of Wear and Tear Allowance

Imagine the same scenario as above, but this time, John is charging £600 monthly rent. He charges an extra £100 because John himself pays the utility bills and gardening services.

The annual income is now therefore £7,200.

John *cannot* offset 10% of £7,200 against his rental profits.

He first has to deduct the costs that would normally be borne by the tenant, which in this case is £100 per month.

Therefore he can only claim 10% on £6,000 (£7,200 – £1,200), which equates to £600.

6.3. Understanding the 'Renewals Basis' Method

Tax Tip - 7
The **renewals basis** method can be used for either a furnished, partly furnished, or even an un-furnished property.

The renewals method allows you to offset the cost of 'renewing' or 'replacing' an item in a property.

Unlike the 10% Wear and Tear Allowance, there are no restrictions as to when this rule can be used.

However, there are some important points to note if you decide to use this method.

a) **You cannot offset the initial cost of an item.**
   This is a *very important* point, and many landlords get into trouble by accidentally overlooking this.

   If you purchase a property and decide to fully furnish it with new or even second-hand items, then you *cannot* offset the cost of providing these furnishings.

   You can only offset the costs of these furnishings when you renew them.

b) **If you use this allowance, then you cannot change between this method and the wear and tear allowance on a yearly basis.**

Here are a couple of case studies to illustrate the use of this rule.

Case Study - 30 : Renewing and Offsetting the Costs

Roy buys a new house and decides to let out his previous main residence.

He leaves the existing furniture in his old house and decides to use the renewals basis method to reduce his income tax liability.

Two years later, he spends £4,000 renewing all the furniture on the property.

This whole amount can be offset against his annual property income tax bill.

More importantly, if by offsetting this whole amount it means that he has made a loss on his property, then the loss can be carried forward into the next tax year.

Case Study - 31 : Be Careful of Initial Costs

Alex buys a brand-new luxury apartment in the city centre.

He decides to fully furnish the property and spends £7,000 on 'kitting it out' with the best furniture and appliances.

He considers using the 'renewals' method but quickly changes his mind after he realises that the initial cost of furnishing can not be offset against his rental income.

Selling items and receiving an income

If you decide to replace an old item and receive some income by either selling it or scrapping it, then the amount received must be taken into account when calculating your tax liability.

You must deduct the amount received (when disposing of the old item) from the amount spent on the new item.

The case study below illustrates this important point.

Case Study - 32 : Considering the Cost of Disposing of the Old Item

Robert decides to replace the sofa in his luxury apartment.

Although the sofa is not in a poor state, he feels that it no longer fits in with the high standards of the apartment.

He advertises the sofa and receives £200 from a buyer.

The replacement sofa costs £1,000.

This means that he can only offset the amount of £800 from his rental income. This is because the income received by selling the old sofa must be deducted from the cost of the new replacement.

6.4. How to Decide Which Method to Use

In this section you will learn how you can decide whether you should use the **10% Wear and Tear Allowance** or the **renewals basis** method.

The table below shows which method you can use for the type of property you are providing.

Type of Property	Renewals Basis	10% Wear and Tear
Fully Furnished	Yes	Yes
Partly Furnished	Yes	No
Unfurnished	Yes	No

It is clear from the above table that if you have a partly furnished or an unfurnished property, then you can only use the renewals basis method.

If you have a fully furnished property, then you have an important decision to make.

Here are some important points that you should consider before you decide which method to use.

a) Consider the cost of fully furnishing a property.

   If you are buying a property and are going to let it out fully furnished, then you *must* consider the cost you are going to incur in initially furnishing it.

   If the cost is going to be high, then it may be better use the 10% Wear and Tear Allowance.

This is purely because

- you will be providing high-quality furnishings and will not expect to replace them for a good few years, i.e., five to seven years.

  Therefore you will have to wait this period of time before you can claim the renewals basis.

- If you decide to sell the property before you renew the furnishings, then by using the renewal basis, you will not have managed to offset any renewals cost against your property. This means that you will have unnecessarily paid more in tax.

However, if you use the 10% Wear and Tear Allowance, then you can claim this from the date you purchased the property.

b) Consider how often you will need to replace the furnishings.

If you believe that you will need to renew the furnishings on a regular basis, i.e., every two to three years, then it may well be beneficial to use the renewals basis.

This may particularly be the case if you are providing accommodation to students.

If you don't expect to replace the furnishings for at least five years, then the 10% Wear and Tear Allowance may be more suited.

c) Consider administration time.

The 10% Wear and Tear Allowance is easy to calculate, and you do not need to keep any receipts for tax purposes.

However, if you decide to use the renewals method, then you will not only need to keep all your receipts (as proof that you have incurred an expense), but you will also need to track and record all these expenditures.

7. Getting to Grips With the Term 'Wholly and Exclusively'

This section will address the term 'wholly and exclusively.'

If you have ever read and tried to digest the Property Income Manual, then you will have noticed that this phrase is consistently mentioned in the guide.

By the time you have finished this section, you will know how to test if an expense satisfies this rule and whether it can be offset against your property rental income.

7.1. Understanding the Term 'Wholly and Exclusively'

> **Tax Tip - 8**
>
> The Inland Revenue states,
>
> **'You can't deduct expenses unless they are incurred wholly and exclusively for business purposes.'**

To put it simply, this statement means that if you incurred an expense that was not used for the purpose of your property, in any way at all, then you cannot offset the cost.

Whenever you incur a cost for your investment property, always ask yourself,

'Has the cost been incurred wholly and exclusively for the property?'

If you can answer **YES** to this question, then it is highly likely you will be able to offset the cost against your property rental income.

7.2. What If Cost is Not Wholly and Exclusively Incurred for Property?

Sometimes you may incur a cost that is not used 'wholly and exclusively' for your property. However, a portion of the cost has been incurred for your property.

For such situations the Inland Revenue provides the following guideline:

> **'Where a definite part or proportion of an expense is wholly and exclusively incurred for the purposes of the business, you can deduct that part or proportion.'**

What this effectively means is that you need to determine what part or proportion of the cost is attributed to your investment property. This is because you cannot offset the entire cost.

The following case study will help to illustrate this guideline.

Case Study - 33 : Where Costs Are Not Wholly and Exclusively Incurred for Property

Bill has an investment property.

The bathroom is looking rather 'tired,' so he decides to re-tile it completely. He goes to a local tile shop, where they have an offer of 12 square metres of tiles for £240.

However, he only requires seven square metres for his investment property.

After some serious head scratching he appreciates that the deal is an excellent value for the money and too good to miss. He therefore purchases the tiles.

He decides to use the extra 5 square metres of tiles in his own house.

This means that the entire cost has not been incurred wholly and exclusively for the property. However, a portion of the cost, i.e., 7/12ths, has been incurred wholly and exclusively for the property.

He may therefore offset £140 (i.e., 7/12ths of £240) against his rental income.

7.3. Costs of Maintenance and Repairs

Tax Tip - 9

Once you have purchased and successfully let your property, any maintenance costs incurred that help prevent the property from deteriorating can be offset against your rental income.

It is very likely that at some point you will have to carry out some maintenance work to keep your property in an acceptable state of repair.

When this happens, you will be able to offset the cost against your property income as long as it satisfies both of the following conditions.

a) **It is not an initial cost.**
An initial cost is one that is incurred after the property is purchased but before a tenant has taken occupation of it.

b) **It is not a capital improvement.**
A capital improvement is when work is carried out that increases the value of the property.

Case Study - 34 : Maintenance Cost

John is informed by his tenants that water is leaking from the upstairs bathroom into the downstairs living room.

He calls a plumber to repair the damaged bathroom water pipe and also hires a painter/decorator to redecorate the damaged ceiling.

The entire cost of the work is £300, and it can be offset against the rental income.

7.4. Typical maintenance/repair costs

The following list details typical maintenance/repair costs that you are likely to incur and which you can offset against your rental income:

- repairing water/gas leaks, burst pipes, etc.;
- repairing electrical faults;
- fixing broken windows, doors, gutters, roof slates/tiles, etc.;
- repairing internal/external walls, roofs, floors, etc.;
- painting and redecorating the property;
- treating damp/rot;
- re-pointing, stone cleaning, etc.;
- hiring equipment to carry out necessary repair work;
- repairing existing fixtures and fittings which include:
    - radiators,
    - boilers,
    - water tanks,
    - bathroom suites,
    - electrical/gas appliances,
    - furniture, and furnishings, etc.

7.5. Initial cost of maintenance/repair

If you carry out maintenance work on a property before you first let it out, then the cost incurred cannot be offset against your rental income.

Case Study - 35 : Initial Maintenance Cost

Fred buys a run-down investment property and spends £5,000 getting the property ready so that is in a habitable condition.

This cost cannot be offset against the rental income as it has been incurred *before* the property has been let.

However, the cost can be offset against any capital gain that he makes when he sells the property.

If you know that your property needs some maintenance work that is not essential, then consider making it after the property has been occupied by a tenant.

By doing this, you will be able to offset the whole cost against the rental income.

Case Study - 36 : Waiting to Make Non-essential Repairs

Fred buys an investment property.

Ideally, he would like to re-decorate the whole property as he feels it is rather outdated. However, he decides to wait until the property has been occupied by tenants before he carries out this work.

The first tenant moves out after a year of occupation.

He then spends £2,000 re-decorating the whole property.

This whole cost can now be offset against the property income. Had he decided to do this work straight after buying the property, then he would have not been able to offset the costs in this way.

7.6. Capital improvements

If you carry out a capital improvement that increases the value of the property, then you *cannot* offset this cost against your rental income.

This is because it is not classed as maintenance or repair work.

Case Study - 37 : Capital Improvements

After years of owning his investment property, Fred applies for, and gets approval to add, a conservatory.

The cost of the conservatory is £20,000.

Because the conservatory has increased the value of the house by £30,000, it cannot be offset against the rental income.

Again, the cost will be offset against any capital gain that he makes when he sells the property.

Tax Tip - 10

REMEMBER: If you have incurred an initial cost or made a capital improvement, then these costs can be claimed when you sell your property.

8. Replacing Your Fixtures and Fittings

This section will help you to understand what is meant by the term **fixtures and fittings** and when you can offset the replacement of them against your income tax.

8.1. What are Fixtures and Fittings?

These are items that are classed as being an integral part of the property. If a new tenant moves into a property, then they will expect these items to be in the property.

Examples of fixtures and fittings include

- windows, doors, light fittings;
- kitchen units;
- bathroom suites;
- gas central heating systems and radiators or hot water supply tanks;
- gas fires, etc.

The most important point to understand about fixtures and fittings is that any cost incurred in repairing them or replacing them with a like-for-like product can be offset against the property rental income. This is regardless of whether the property is un-furnished, partly furnished, or fully furnished.

For the remainder of this section we will focus on the replacement of fixtures and fittings.

Two important conditions must be satisfied before you can offset the cost of replacing fixtures and fittings. These are the following.

a) The cost must be a 'replacement' cost. In other words, it cannot be for the installation of fixtures and fittings that were not previously in the property.

b) The cost must be for a similar, like-for-like product.

If both these conditions are met, then the cost can be deducted from the rental profits.

8.2. Replacing Fixtures and Fittings

Whenever you decide to replace existing fixtures and fittings, they are likely to fall into one of the following three categories:

a) like-for-like replacement;
b) like-for-like replacement but with capital improvements;
c) replacement with superior fixtures and fittings.

Each of the above scenarios is treated differently when it comes to calculating your income tax bill, and each is illustrated in the following sections.

8.2.1. *Like-for-like replacement*

If you replace existing fixtures and fittings with similar like-for-like products, then the entire cost can be offset against the income tax bill.

Case Study - 38 : Replacing With Like-for-Like (1)

Alex has been renting out his buy-to-let property for seven years and decides that it is now time to change the bathroom suite.

He finds a similar bathroom suite of comparable quality that costs £500. The cost of having the old suite removed and the new one fitted is also £500.

This means that the entire project costs £1,000.

This whole amount can be offset against the annual rental income.

8.2.2. *What if it is not possible to replace with like-for-like?*

The Inland Revenue appreciates that it is not possible to replace with a like-for-like product in all instances. This is especially true if you are replacing something that is several years old as a like-for-like product may no longer be available.

In such circumstances, it is possible to replace with a superior item, especially if it is of a similar cost.

Case Study - 39 : Replacing With Like-for-Like (2)

Alex also decides to replace the wooden, single-glazed windows as they are starting to rot. The windows are more than 10 years old.

The cost of replacing with similar single-glazed windows is £3,500, and this includes the fitting and removal of the old, rotten windows.

However, the cost of replacing the windows with UPVC double-glazed windows is actually cheaper and costs £3,400. This price also includes the fitting and removal of the old windows.

Although the UPVC double-glazed windows are of a superior quality, the Inland Revenue accepts that these types of windows are the 'standard' in all new build properties.

Therefore it is possible to use these as replacements and offset the entire cost incurred.

8.2.3. *Like-for-like replacement but with capital improvements*

If you replace the existing fixtures and fittings with a like-for-like product but also make a capital improvement, then you can only offset the cost of the like-for-like replacement.

Case Study - 40 : Replacing With Like-for-Like but With Capital Improvement

Alex also decides to replace the kitchen units.

The cost of replacing the kitchen units with like-for-like replacements is £1,600. However, he has some additional space that he wishes to utilise, so he orders an additional three units at a cost of £600.

Alex is able to offset the cost of the £1,600 like-for-like replacement against his rental income.

However, the additional three units are treated as a capital improvement, and this cost cannot be offset against the rental income.

Instead, the cost of the additional units can be offset against any capital gain arising when the property is sold.

8.2.4. *Replacement with superior fixtures and fittings*

If you decide to replace existing fixtures and fittings with totally superior ones, then the cost of these cannot be offset against the rental income. Instead, they will be offset against any capital gain arising when the property is sold.

Case Study - 41 : Replacing With Superior Fixtures and Fittings

John decides to replace the bathroom suite in his investment property.

Replacing with a like-for-like suite would cost £1,300. However, he decides that in the future he will move into this property himself, so he buys a much more superior and expensive bathroom. At the same time he also decides to re-tile the bathroom.

The cost of this mini-project is £4,000, and it adds approximately £6,000 to the value of the house.

Tax specialists have differing view on how this could be handled.

You could offset the £1,300 against the rental income and the remaining £2,700 against the capital gain. Alternatively the entire cost can be classed as a 'capital cost' and you could therefore offset the whole £4,000 against the capital gains.

9. Other Ways to Reduce Your Income Tax Bill

In the strategies to date you have learned about the common costs that can be offset against the rental income.

In this section you will now become familiar with numerous other typical costs that a property investor is likely to incur and that can be offset against the rental income.

9.1. Rents, Rates, and Insurance

The following costs are incurred by property investors when the property is let or when the property is empty and between lets.

9.1.1. Rents

The most common type of rent that an investor is likely to incur is ground rent. Landlords are liable to pay this rent on any leasehold property/land, and therefore any such expenditure can be offset against the rental income.

9.1.2. Rates

If you decide to pay any of the following rates on your property, then they can be offset against the rental income:

- water;
- electricity;
- gas;
- council tax;
- service charges;
- TV licence;
- telephone line rental;
- satellite TV charges, etc.

9.1.3. Insurance

Any insurance premiums that you pay for your properties or products/services relating to your property can also be offset against the rental income.

The most common premiums you are likely to pay will include the following:

- building insurance;
- contents insurance;
- insurance cover for service supplies such as
    - gas central heating,
    - plumbing insurance,
    - electrical insurance;
- insurance cover for appliances such as
    - washer/dryer,
    - fridge/freezer,
    - television, etc.

9.2. Can I Offset Pre-trading Expenditure?

Ian McTernan answers this commonly asked question as follows:

'This is a bit of a grey area as far as taxation goes.

The rules for pre-trading expenditure are quite complex, but in theory you can claim expenses incurred in the seven years before commencement of the rental 'business.'

The expenses are treated as incurred on the first day the rental 'business' starts.

Having said that, the Revenue will want to examine these expenses closely with a view to establishing whether they were incurred 'wholly and exclusively' for the purposes of the 'trade.'

Again in theory the Revenue can disallow any expense which has a duality of purpose, but in practice they will usually allow a split to be made.

They will also examine the expenses to see whether they are capital or revenue in nature.

Below is a list of some common types of pre-trading expenditure you are likely to incur before you buy your property:

- travelling costs (see section Travelling Costs);
- the cost of purchasing dedicated trade/magazines for helping you to find your property;
- the cost of telephone calls when phoning estate agents/property vendors, etc.

The important point to note is that each occurrence of a pre-trading expenditure must be incurred wholly and exclusively for the property.'

9.3. Carrying Over Rental Losses

Tax Tip - 11

Any rental losses made on a property can be carried forward into the next financial year.

Sometimes you will incur a rental loss on your property investment. Rental losses can be incurred intentionally or unintentionally. The important point to note is that any losses can be carried forward into the next year and can be used to reduce your tax liability for that year.

Case Study - 42 : Carrying Over Rental Losses

After three years of owning his two-bedroom buy-to-let property, John decides to replace the bathroom suite. The cost of replacing it with a like-for-like replacement is £2,500.

His rental income for the property is £4,800 annually, but after all his annual expenses are deducted, e.g., offsetting interest payments, the cost of the replacement bathroom suite, etc., he is left with a £1,000 rental loss.

This loss can be carried forward and offset against his rental income the following year.

9.4. Travelling Costs

You are likely to incur travelling costs when you use either your car or public transport for travelling to and from your property.

Both methods are detailed below.

9.4.1. Car petrol usage

Ian McTernan states that you can claim for the cost of travel to and from the property, provided the trip was wholly for a business purpose.

Claiming a mileage allowance is better and easier than the apportionment method[2] as this is just a question of working out how many miles it is and then claiming 40 pence per mile for the first 10,000 and then 25 pence thereafter.

You must be able to prove the trip was purely for a business purpose, though!

Therefore it important that you keep a log of the mileage that you have done for the purpose of your property. For each trip, make sure you keep a log of the following:

- the date the trip was made;
- the purpose of the trip (e.g., visit tenant, carry out maintenance repairs, etc.);
- the miles that were travelled.

[2]The apportionment method involves keeping a log of the annual car mileage and all the expenditures that have been incurred on the car (including petrol receipts). You determine how many miles were for the purpose of your property business and then apportion the expenditure accordingly.

Case Study - 43 : Claiming Car Mileage Allowance

John has been renting his property for three years and then decides to renovate/re-decorate the entire property.

He dos the work himself and spends two weeks travelling to and from the property, which is 15 miles from his home. He also has to go to various DIY retailers to buy his materials.

Over the two week period he travels 800 miles, which are wholly and exclusively for the purpose of his property.

In addition to this, he travels an additional 200 miles visiting the property and the tenants at various times.

This means that over the entire year he has travelled 1,000 miles.

Therefore he can offset £400 (i.e., 1,000 miles × 40 pence per mile) against his rental income.

9.4.2. Public transport

If you use a bus, train, or even aeroplane (for overseas investors) to travel to your property, then you can again offset the cost, as long as the trip is wholly and exclusively for the purpose of the property.

Please note that you must keep your receipts as proof of your trip.

If your visit is dual purpose, i.e., you are going on holiday but are also looking at the property market, then you cannot claim the cost.

9.4.3. Travelling costs for overseas property

With the growing trend of overseas investors, a common question asked is:

Can I offset the cost of travelling overseas to look at potential investments against my UK rental income?

The answer to this is that you **cannot** offset the overseas travel cost against the UK properties, as the expense is not connected with them.

Case Study - 44 : Travelling costs for overseas property

Jennifer has a portfolio of properties in the UK but now decides to invest in Spain. She arranges a trip to Spain to look at a number of investment properties. The total cost of the trip is £500. She cannot offset the cost of the trip against the income from her UK properties.

9.5. General Property Costs

If you have a portfolio or properties and incur expenses then it may not be possible to attribute the cost to a single property. This is because the expenditure may have been for all of the properties.

A good example of this is when purchasing decorating materials for a property. In such circumstances you can either:

- apportion the cost against the properties, or
- have a separate listing of generic expenses to add on at the end when you combine all the incomes and expenditures.

Either way is fine, as it makes no difference to the tax position, though practically the latter option may be easier and simpler to implement.

9.6. Storage Costs

A cost incurred by an increasing number of investors is storage costs.

The cost of renting storage space is allowable against rental income. The reason is that it fulfils the principal criteria of "wholly and exclusively", as the cost was incurred for the purpose of your property business. If you never had rented property then you would not be incurring such costs.

Case Study - 45 : Storage Costs

John owns 5 properties which are all fully furnished. However he finds a new long-term tenant for his property who has his own furniture and furnishings. John decides that he will empty the property and store the furniture in rented storage. The cost of rental storage is £450. This amount can be offset against the rental income as it has been incurred 'wholly and exclusively' for the purpose of the rental business.

9.7. Other Common Landlord Expenditures

Below is a list of other common costs that a landlord will incur that can be offset against the rental income:

- safety certificates, e.g., gas and electrical safety;
- stationery, e.g., stamps, envelopes, books;
- computer equipment;
- bad debts;
- legal and professional costs, e.g., accountancy costs;
- service costs, e.g., window cleaner, gardener;
- furniture/appliance rentals;
- advertisement costs;
- letting agent costs;
- books, magazines, etc;
- security/smoke alarms;
- telephone calls, including mobile telephone bills (but make sure you have an itemised bill to prove the calls made);
- bank charges (e.g., interest charged on property bank account).

9.8. Can I Offset the Cost of a £5,000 Property Seminar?

With the property investment boom a large number of potential and inexperienced investors have been attending seminars and paying thousands of pounds for learning about various property investment techniques.

A common question that arises is whether the cost of the seminar can be offset against any future income tax bill.

When asked the question **'Can I offset the cost of a £5,000 property seminar?,'** Arthur Weller provides the following guidance:

If the cost of the seminar is wholly and exclusively for the purposes of the trade presently carried out by the taxpayer, then it is allowable.

Here is what the Inland Revenue has to say about the matter:

> ***'Expenditure on training courses attended by the proprietor of a business with the purpose of up-dating his or her skills and professional expertise is normally revenue expenditure, which is deductible from profits of the business provided it is incurred wholly and exclusively for the purposes of the trade or profession carried on by the individual at the time the training is undertaken'.***

So what exactly does that mean?

Already a property investor
If you are already a property investor, with a portfolio, and attend the course to update your investment skills, then you can offset the entire cost.

You can offset the cost as you will be regarded as updating your skills.

Case Study - 46 : When You CAN Offset the Cost of a £5,000 Property Course

Bill has been investing in property since the early 1980s and has built a portfolio of 12 properties.

However, in 1999 he decides take property investment more seriously and attends a £5,000 course to update and sharpen his investment skills so that he can focus on emerging areas for investment.

The entire cost of the course can be offset against his rental income.

New to property investment
However, if you want to start investing in property and attend a course to learn how to do this, then you will not be able to offset the costs against the rental income.

You cannot offset the cost as you will not be 'updating' your skills in your current profession.

Case Study - 47 : When You CANNOT Offset the Cost of a £5,000 Property Course

Following the collapse of the stock market, John decides that the only way he will be able to maintain his lifestyle when he retires is if he invests in property.

So, in 2001 he attends a property investment course to learn all about property investment. Shortly after the course he buys his first investment property.

The cost of the course cannot be offset against any future rental income.

A word of warning
If you do decide to make a claim, it could well trigger an investigation.

The Inland Revenue does keep a close eye on large amounts being claimed, so be warned!

9.9. Capital Allowances for landlords

If you decide to purchase a piece of equipment or an asset that is used for the purpose of the business then you can claim a 25% annual depreciation allowance.

Examples of such assets include:

- Computers and office furniture (that you use in your own home for running the business)
- Tools for maintaining upkeep of properties i.e. DIY tools
- Vehicles (please note that this is restricted to the lower of 25% of the unrelieved balance or £3,000).

The depreciation allowance can be claimed annually until the equipment/asset is disposed of.

Here are a couple of examples that show how the 25% depreciation allowance works.

Case Study - 48 : Capital Allowances for Assets

Wasim has a portfolio of five investment properties. He also carries out much of the maintenance and repairs on the properties himself, so he decides to purchase professional DIY toolkit for £150 in March 2002.

The annual depreciation allowance is calculated as follows:

Tax Year	Toolkit Value	Annual 25% Allowance
2001-2002	£150	£37.50
2002-2003	£112.5	£28.13
2003-2004	£84.37	£21.09
2004-2005	£63.28	£15.82
etc..		

As you can see from the above example, the amount that can be claimed on an annual basis continues to decrease as the toolkit value decreases.

Case Study - 49 : Capital Allowances for a Vehicle

Wasim also buys a new car for £15,000 in March 2004. The car is primarily used for his private use but he also uses it for the purpose of his property portfolio. For example he uses the car whenever visiting the property and for all other property associated travelling.

Over the year, he travels 10,000 miles in the car and 2,000 of this is connected with travelling associated with his property portfolio.

This means that 20% of the use of the car has been for Wasim's property business. We now need to determine whether to use 25% of the unrelieved balance, or the fixed £3,000 to determine the amount that Wasim can claim.

If we calculate the 25% of the car value (£15,000) in the 2003-2004 tax year then this equals £3,750. This means that we need to use the fixed value of £3,000 as this is the lower of the two applicable values.

Therefore Wasim can claim 20% of £3,000 which equals £600 in the 2003-2004 tax-year.

In the 2005-2006 tax year if the car is again used 20% for the purposes of his property business then the unrelieved balance of the car will be £12,000 (i.e. £15,000 - £3,000). This time if we calculate 25% of the unrivalled balance then it equals £3,000, which is the same as the fixed allowance. This means that again Wasim can claim a £600 capital allowance deduction against his rental income.

Note: If the capital allowance is used then you cannot also use the 40p per mileage claimed in section 9.4.1 Car petrol usage.

Also, this method of depreciation cannot be used for fittings, fixtures and furniture that are supplied within a residential property.

10. The Two Ways to Calculate your UK Property Rental Income Profits

Most landlords (and even some accountants) are unaware that there are two methods that can be used to calculate your annual UK property income tax. These methods are known as **'Cash Basis'** and **'Earnings Basis'**.

In this article we will explain when and how both methods can be used.

To demonstrate each of the methods the following case study will be used:

Louise owns one buy-to-let property, which generate an annual rental income of £12,000. The rent is paid six months in advance and runs from 1st January 2004 till 31st December 2004.

This means that she receives £6,000 in rental income on 1st January 2004 and £6,000 on 1st July 2004. The 1st January 2004 rental income covers the period 1st January to 30th June and the 1st July 2004 rental income covers 1st July to 31st December.

She also has some roof repairs carried out in the property in March 2004. The cost for the work done is £1,000. However the builder is a little slow in billing and he does not raise the invoice till May 2004 which Louise promptly pays.

10.1. Cash Basis

The cash basis can be used when the income generated from your property rental business (before allowable expenses are deducted) do not exceed £15,000 in the tax year.

When the cash basis is used, the income tax calculation is based on when the rent was actually **received** and when expenditures were **paid**. Note here that the emphasis in this method is on **'received'** and **'Paid'**. In other words it is based on when money exchanges hands.

When she completes her tax return the rental income will attributed to the tax years as follows:

<u>Rental Income Received</u>
2003-2004 tax year rental income is £6,000. This is because the first payment of 1st January 2004 lies in this tax year.

2004-2005 tax year rental income is also £6,000. This is because the second payment of 1st July 2004 lies in this tax year.

<u>Expenditure Incurred</u>
The roof repair work was carried out in the 2003-2004 tax year, as it was carried out in March 2004. However the invoice was not paid till the following tax year. This means that Louise will only be able to offset the expenditure against the 2004-2005 tax year as this is when the invoice was paid i.e. May 2004.

10.2. Comments about the Cash Basis

The Inland Revenue gives the following conditions in paragraph 91 of the IR150 Manual.

We are, therefore, prepared to accept the use of a 'cash basis' (profits based on the cash paid and received in the year) provided all the following conditions are met:

- the case is small; by a 'small' case we mean one where, for any year, the total gross receipts of your rental business (before allowable expenses are deducted) don't exceed £15,000; and
- the 'cash basis' is used consistently; and
- the result is reasonable overall and does not differ substantially from the strict 'earnings basis'

10.3. Earnings Basis

The earnings basis is also sometimes referred to as the 'accruals basis' and follows ordinary commercial accounting methods. When using this, method there are two very important points to note:

Firstly – You can use this method regardless of whether the income generated from your property rental business (before allowable expenses are deducted) exceeds £15,000 in the tax year. In other words if you annual rental income is below £15,000 per year then you can still use this method. However if it is above £15,000 then you must use this method.

Secondly - The income tax calculation is based on when the period the rental income **arises** and when expenditures were **incurred**. Note here that the emphasis in this method is on '**arises'** and **'incurred'** which is different to the cash basis method.

Lets continue with the case study:

When she completes her tax return the rental income will attributed to the tax years as follows.

Rental Income Received

As we know, £6,000 was paid for the first six months that the tenant lived in the property. The upfront £6,000 payment on the 1st January 2004 was to cover the period 1st January to 30th June. However, this payment covered both the 2003-2004 and 2004-2005 tax years.

Therefore the £6,000 rental income needs to be apportioned across both tax years, as the rental income attributable from 1st January to 5th April will be recorded against the 2003-2004 tax year and the income attributable from 6th April to 2oth June to the 2004-2005 tax year.

Here is how the apportionment could be done:

Daily Rental Income

£6,000 was due for 181 days (i.e. 1st Jan to 30th June).

This means that the amount charged per day = £6,000 / 181 = £33.15

Rental income for 2003-2004 tax year
The number of days from 1st January to 5th April inclusive = 95 days, and 95 * £33.15 = £3149.25.

Therefore £3,149 is attributable to and recorded against the 2003-2004 tax year.

Rental income for 2003-2004 tax year
The remaining rental income from 6th April to 30th June is attributed to the 2004-2005 tax year. This amount is £2,850.75.

Also, the entire rental income of £6,000 that is paid on 1st July is also attributed to the 2004-2005 tax year. This is because it cover the period 1st July to 31st December. This entire period sits within the 2004-2005 tax year.

Expenditure Incurred
Even though the payment for the roof repair work made in May 2004, the work was actually carried out in March 2004. This means that because March falls within 2003-2004 tax year the £1,000 cost will be attributed to this tax year.

As you can see it is beneficial to offset the cost in this tax year rather than waiting till the following tax year.

Comments about the Earnings Basis

Here are some important points to note when using this method.

- This method must be used if your gross income exceeds £15,000 per tax year. However you can also decide to use it even if your income is less than £15,000.

- In the case study we calculated the amount due for the five odd days in April. The Inland revenue does allow a concession here to simplify the computation. The concession allows you to ignore the split if you do it consistently across both income and expenditures and the figures are small. The strict daily apportionment is required when the figures are 'substantial'. Please note that there is no indication given by the 'Inland Revenue' as to what is meant by 'substantial'.

- As you have seen here we are not working on the basis of what was **paid** or **received**. Therefore if a tenant did not actually pay the rental income that was due then you would create a bad debt to offset this against the rental income.

Companies and Property Taxes

11. Can a Limited Company Improve YOUR Tax Position?

In this section you will learn whether holding your properties through a company will benefit your tax position.

11.1. The Most Commonly Asked Tax Questions

'Should I buy my property through a limited company?'

'Should I move my properties into a limited company?'

'Is it true that I can save tax by holding my properties in a limited company?'

I am sure that, like most investors, you will have either asked or been involved in a discussion where these questions have been debated.

In all fairness, the answer to these kinds of questions depends on the following three key factors:

a) your chosen investment strategy;
b) your personal and financial circumstances/ambitions;
c) how long you intend to hold on to the properties.

However, before you even decide whether a limited company will improve your tax position, there are some very basic rules and guidelines that must be understood.

11.2. Transferring Properties Into a Limited Company

Do you already own investment properties?

Are you already on the buy-to-let investment ladder?

If the answer is yes, and you are now considering whether moving your properties into a limited company will save you tax, then consider the following FACT:

Properties must be transferred into a Limited Company at market value, unless a portfolio exists that is deemed to constitute a 'business'.

Yes, that's right!

Generally speaking, moving properties into a company is treated in the same way as if you were selling the properties.

If you bought your investment property five years ago and you would now like to move it into a limited company, then you are likely to have to pay an *immediate* capital gains tax liability.

This is due to the fact that property prices have significantly increased over the past few years.

The exception to this rule is if the property is your **principle private residence**.

Case Study - 50 : Transferring Properties Into a Limited Company

Alex bought five investment properties between 1992 and 1996.

Their combined purchase value was £250,000.

In 2004 they are worth a combined total of £550,000; that is, the combined value of his portfolio has more than doubled!

This means that his capital gain is £300,000.

By transferring the properties into a company, he may be liable to pay 40% tax on this amount, which means that he will have an immediate tax liability of £120,000 (excluding any reliefs) if he is a higher-rate taxpayer.

Tax Tip - 12

Do not start to form a limited company before you know what your tax liability will be.

11.3. Understanding 'Limited Liability'

There is a common misunderstanding by many property investors who believe that if they hold their properties in a limited company, they will escape from the banks/creditors if anything goes wrong.

Ian McTernan, author of the guide 'How to use companies to avoid property taxes,' helps to explain when the Limited Liability status *will* and *will not* protect you.

As a separate legal entity, the company is, in theory, responsible for its own debts and liabilities. However, it is *very likely* that any lender will insist on a personal guarantee from the directors or shareholders when lending to the company. This means that if the company fails, the directors *will be liable*!

Consider the following case study.

Case Study - 51 : When Limited Liability Will Not Help You

Mr. and Mrs. Prone form the limited company ABC Ltd. They borrow 75% of the purchase price and proceed to rent out the property through the company. They withdraw every penny of rent received without considering any tax consequences.

At the end of the first year the mortgage company decides to repossess the property as the mortgage has not been paid for six months.

In the above case study the directors will be held responsible for paying

- the outstanding mortgage;
- corporation tax on the profits;
- any tax due on the money that they have withdrawn.

This is because the liabilities have arisen as a direct result of their actions.

By law, directors are largely responsible for the actions of the company, and hence if it all goes wrong, there is a fair chance that the directors will find themselves personally liable for any debts arising as a result of their decisions.

However, having the cover of **limited liability** can still be useful if the business incurs unexpected (i.e., outside the control of the directors) losses or liabilities.

Such losses and liabilities can occur when

- a property development goes horribly wrong;
- tenants refuse to move out, and the company runs out of cash to pay the mortgage;
- interest rates suddenly double;
- the housing market crashes (let's hope this doesn't happen!);
- a tenant is injured on your property and successfully sues the company for personal injury.

This last pointer is a very good reason for ensuring that you have the correct landlord's insurance in place.

Let's look at another case study to illustrate the point.

Case Study - 52 : Using Limited Liability to Your Advantage

Mr. and Mrs. Prone decide to enter the buy-to-let market and set up a limited company to hold the property. The property costs £100,000, and a loan is obtained from the bank for 85% of the purchase price.

Tenants are found and a rental agreement signed. No insurance is taken out as it is not considered a priority.

Three months later, a solicitor's letter arrives claiming that the tenant has fallen down the stairs as a result of improper maintenance of the stairways (there is a hole in one of the stairs).

After much debate and a court case, compensation is set at £150,000. The directors are cleared of any responsibility in the case by the judge. Clearly, the company cannot pay this amount of money, and the company is put into liquidation.

In the above case study the owners have been successful in that the limited liability of the company has saved them from being personally responsible for the costs.

If this had not been in place, then the costs would have fallen on them, which would have resulted in them having to sell their own houses to meet the claim.

11.4. Three Major Tax Benefits of Using a Limited Company

Tax Tip - 13

As a general rule, if you intend to re-invest the money you have made through your property investments, e.g., you want to continue re-investing the profits into acquiring more properties, then it will be beneficial to invest through a limited company.

There are two *significant* tax benefits of growing a property portfolio through a company. These are explained below.

a) Lower-rate tax savings.

   As a higher-rate taxpayer, you pay 40% on your profit and gains. For a limited company the tax rates are between 19% and 30% — a considerable savings.

b) Stamp duty savings.

   You only pay stamp duty at a rate of 0.5% when purchasing company shares[3]. Other Benefits/Drawbacks of a Limited Company

[3] This only applies when purchasing a company that already owns the property. It does not apply when a company purchases a property.

11.4.1. Benefits

Here are some more favourable tax benefits to consider when deciding whether to own your properties through a limited company.

- A company can define its own accounting period that does not exceed 12 months.

- Indexation relief is still available for any capital gains.

- You will see lower tax rates as companies pay tax between 19% and 30%.

- Properties can be transferred within companies without incurring a tax liability[4].

- You can grow a portfolio more quickly within a company by continuing to re-invest the profits, thus deferring any tax.

- Dividends can be extracted from a company in a tax efficient way.

11.4.2. Drawbacks

Here are some drawbacks that you should consider before deciding to own your properties through a limited company.

- Companies cannot use the annual personal CGT allowance. This allowance is £8,800 for the tax year 2006–2007.

- Official company accounts must be produced. The cost of drawing up such accounts can be three to four times more expensive than having your sole trader accounts drawn up.

- Banks are less reluctant to lend money if you are purchasing through a company.

---

[4]This only applies in a group situation, e.g., a holding company with a 75% subsidiary or subsidiaries.

12. How to Use a Property Management Company to Save Income Tax

The previous section gave an insight into the tax implications of owning your properties through a limited company.

In this section we have featured an article written by James Bailey in the March 2006 edition of Tax Insider (www.taxinsder.co.uk). In this article he considers whether it is still beneficial to use a property management company following the changes to the previous nil-rate tax band.

12.1. Will a Property Management Company Save me Tax?

The article is titled: **Property Management Companies – Are They Still Going to Help Slash your Property Tax Bills?**

> Late last year, the Chancellor announced that the 0% starting rate of corporation tax (CT) for small companies would be abolished from April 2006, and all such companies would pay CT at 19% on all their profits up to £300,000.One of the reasons for this change of heart was the way that small companies were being used to reduce their tax bills by property investors.
>
> Consider the following case study:
>
> Say you own half a dozen properties, which produce gross rents of £60,000 a year, and a rental profit of £40,000 after expenses. Depending on your circumstances, you will be paying income tax at 40% on at least part of this profit – let's say, on £10,000 of it. You set up a company to manage the rentals. It does not own the properties – it charges you a fee for managing them, in the same way any other letting agency or estate agent might.
>
> A typical "arm's length" property management fee is between 10% and 15% of the rents received, so if we take 15%, the company will charge you £9,000 for collecting your £60,000 rents. This reduces your income tax by £3,600 (£9,000 times 40%). The company pays no CT because its profits are below the £10,000 threshold. It will probably cost about £600 per year to run the company (accountant's fees, etc.) so you have saved £3,000.
>
> Getting the money out of the company requires a little more ingenuity; is it still worth it if the company is paying CT at 19%?
>
> If you are a basic rate taxpayer, the answer is probably no – the difference between the basic rate of income tax (22%) and CT at 19% will probably be swallowed up by the cost of running the company. If you pay tax at 40%, it is still worth considering.
>
> On the figures we used above, you still save £3,600 income tax. The company pays CT at 19% on its profits of £8,400 (£9,000 fees, less £600 running costs), so the CT due is £1,596. Taking the running costs into account, the saving is now £1,404 (income tax saved = £3,600, less CT due £1,596 and running costs £600). If you want to get the money out of the company, you have a choice; you can pay yourself dividends, but as a higher rate taxpayer your effective rate

of income tax on these will be 25%. Looking at our company again, it will have cash of £6,804 after paying its expenses and its CT. If you pay that out as a dividend, £1,701 income tax will be due, so you will have saved nothing.

If, however, you liquidate the company after running it for at least two years, business asset taper relief will reduce the capital gain you make on the shares by 75%. On 2005/06 figures, this would mean that a gain of up to £34,000 will be covered by your annual exempt amount for CGT (£34,000 reduced by 75% = £8,500), so there will be no further tax to pay. Which goes to show that although a property management company can still save you some money, it would be pretty borderline unless your rentals were approaching the £100,000 per year mark. Above those levels, however, it is still worth considering.

A word of warning – the strategy of liquidating a company to get the cash out free of tax is "provocative" (that is tax adviser's jargon for "it makes tax inspectors very cross") – you can't do it too often, and you **must** have advice from a tax specialist to avoid getting into trouble with the taxman!

12.2. Draw Up Formal Contracts Between You and Your Company

> **Tax Tip - 14**
> *Do not* set up a company that manages your properties and just simply start paying money into it.

If you just go ahead and start making payments into your company, then the Inland Revenue could challenge you (if you are ever investigated) for making artificial transactions to avoid paying tax.

If you find that by using a property management company you will improve your tax position, then it is advisable to draw up a simple contract between you and your company.

Just drawing up a simple contract that outlines the services your company is providing to you will help to prevent such a challenge!

12.3. Beware of Artificial Transactions!

Arthur Weller advises that you need to be careful and make sure that you are not creating artificial transactions that are aimed at avoiding tax.

In order words, the payments that you make to the company must be realistic and believable by the taxman.

For example, if you have a single property, then you can't pay £750 a month for property management–related charges. It is just not believable, and if you are ever investigated, then the taxman will for sure question whether you were making artificial transactions to avoid paying tax.

You must therefore pay an amount into a company that is believable and relates to the property. A good guide for you is to charge what a letting agent normally charges for their services. So, if your property management company charges you about 15% of your rental income, then this is both realistic and believable.

So, this means that

- for a rental income of £400pcm you can pay your company £60pcm;

- for rental income of £800pcm you can pay your company £120pcm;

- for rental income of £1,200pcm you can pay your company £180pcm.

Stamp Duty Land & Property Tax

13. Saving on Stamp Duty

In this section you will understand when you are liable to pay stamp duty. Generally speaking, anybody purchasing land or property is liable to pay stamp duty up to the rate of 4% on the purchase price of the property.

13.1. When Do Property Investors Pay Stamp Duty?

The two most common scenarios when property investors are liable to pay stamp duty are when

a) land or property is purchased where the purchase price is above £125,000;

b) land or property is transferred where the mortgage amount is greater than £125,000.

> **Tax Tip - 15**
> There is no stamp duty liability if the purchase price or the outstanding mortgage transferred is less than £125,000.

Having witnessed sharp property price increases over the past few years, the government decided to increase the exempt stamp duty threshold from £60,000 to £125,000. This is because it was becoming increasingly unlikely that you would be able to avoid paying stamp duty.

The following table provides details of the current rates of stamp duty.

Purchase Price or Outstanding Mortgage Value	Stamp Duty
Up to £125,000	0%
£125,001–250,000	1%
£250,001–500,000	3%
Greater than £500,000	4%

13.1.1. Stamp duty when buying new land or property

When purchasing land or property, you will be liable to pay stamp duty before you have completed the deal. Typically, the solicitor acting on your behalf in the transaction will include this tax liability in his final invoice to you.

Case Study - 53 : Stamp Duty When Buying Land

Haleema goes to an auction and successfully manages to acquire a small plot of land for £165,000.

She is liable to pay stamp duty at a rate of 1% o this land.

This means that she a stamp duty tax liability of £1,650.

Case Study - 54 : Stamp Duty When Purchasing a New Property

Howard takes his first step onto the property ladder by moving out of his parents home.

He buys a property for £210,000.

The solicitor acting on his behalf calculates that the stamp duty liability is £2,100. He includes this charge in the final invoice that he sends to Howard.

13.1.2. Stamp duty when transferring a property

What a lot of investors fail to realise is that if you transfer ownership of a property to another party (including husband/wife), then stamp duty will be liable if the property is mortgaged and the mortgage amount being transferred is over £125,000.

If the property is not mortgaged and ownership is being gifted, then there is no stamp duty liability.

Case Study - 55 : Stamp Duty When Transferring Property

This case study continues from the previous case study, where Howard has now purchased his property and already incurred a charge of £2,100 in stamp duty.

Two years after the purchase, he marries his long-term girlfriend Betty. He decides to move the property into joint names, where they will have equal 50:50 ownership of the property.

The outstanding amount on the mortgage at the time of transfer is £200,000. By transferring the mortgage into joint names, Betty will not be liable to pay any additional stamp duty tax as the transferred amount of £100,000 (her 50% share) is below the £125,000 stamp duty threshold.

13.2. Stamp Duty Exemption for Deprived Areas

If you are a budding property investor looking to invest in areas of regeneration, then you may well benefit from having no stamp duty liability when buying a property.

This is because the Inland Revenue has designated over 2,000 deprived areas throughout the UK as being exempt from stamp duty. If you purchase a property in one of these areas, then you will not have to pay stamp duty, unless the purchase price exceeds £150,000.

The Inland Revenue states that

> *'The areas that qualify for the relief are the most deprived, as determined by the indices of deprivation in each of the four nations that comprise the United Kingdom. In England and Scotland the poorest 15% of wards and post codes qualify. In Wales and Northern Ireland the poorest 42% of wards are designated as disadvantaged.'*

If you want to check whether a property you are considering purchasing is in a disadvantaged area, click on the link below to use the disadvantaged areas relief search tool.

http://www.hmrc.gov.uk/so/pcode_search.htm

13.3. Stamp Duty Loophole Closed

It was only a matter of time before the Inland Revenue closed a stamp duty loophole that so many people have been using for many years.

The loophole was that homebuyers and property investors would pay over the odds for fixtures and fittings in a house.

This was done to bring the cost of the actual house purchase down so that stamp duty could be dramatically reduced.

Here is a case study to demonstrate what people have been doing.

Case Study - 56 : Avoiding Stamp Duty

John sees a property advertised for £270,000. He loves the house and wants to buy it. The vendor accepts his offer of £265,000. However, this price means that he will have to pay £7,950 in stamp duty tax (i.e., stamp duty is due at a rate of 3%).

He is also interested in buying some fixtures and fittings, which are valued at £2,000. This means that he owes the vendor a total of £267,000.

However, he agrees with the vendor that he will pay £18,000 for the fixtures and fittings.

Therefore he will now only pay £249,000 for the house.

By doing this, John has brought himself into a lower stamp duty tax band and is now only liable to pay £2,490 in stamp duty tax.

This means that he has saved £5460 in stamp duty tax!

In the case study you can see how easily John was able to make a huge tax saving.

13.3.1. Inland Revenue anti-avoidance measure

Stamp duty rules and regulations have changed from 1 December 2003.

Homebuyers will now need to complete a self-assessment land transaction return form and send it to the Inland Revenue. The form will give full details of the sale of the property.

This means that the Inland Revenue will now know exactly how much was paid for the house and its fixtures and fittings, etc. This in turn means that the Inland Revenue will be scrutinising very, very closely all transactions that occur around the stamp duty threshold levels.

Also, the Inland Revenue will be able to investigate the sale for up to 9 months after the filing date of the return, which is 30 days after the transaction.

This means that you may well end up with an unexpected tax bill if they become suspicious of any transactions! Chas Roy-Chowdhury, head of taxation at the Association of Chartered Certified Accountants (ACCA), says that

> ***'Over time thousands of homebuyers whose property was sold for a figure close to a stamp duty threshold may find that the sale comes under the microscope.'***

So, think twice before you consider using the old stamp duty avoidance method!

Other Property Investment Strategies

14. Tax-Free Income for Renting Out Part of Your Home

In this section you will learn about generous annual tax-free savings that are available if you rent out part of your main home.

This tax relief is known as the **rent-a-room** relief.

14.1. What is the Rent-a-Room Relief?

If you decide to let a room in your main residence, you can receive a rental income of up to £4,250 and have no tax liability[5].

In order to claim this allowance, the property must satisfy the following conditions:

a) you must also live in the property;

b) the room you are letting out must be fully furnished.

If you claim the rent-a-room relief, then it is not possible to claim any expenditure that you have incurred with regards to the letting.

This is a very common strategy for those people who have houses that are too large for their needs. For example, if your children have left home, then you may decide to rent the room they lived in for an additional tax-free income.

Case Study - 57 : Rent-a-Room Relief (1)

Bill and Mary have a three-bedroom detached house. They are both higher-rate taxpayers.

Their daughter Louise leaves home and moves in with her long-term boyfriend, so they decide to let her room out to a local teacher.

They receive an annual rental income of £4,000 per annum.

There is no tax liability on this income as it is below the £4,250 threshold value.

If the income received is greater than the annual allowance, then tax is liable on the amount above this value.

[5] All that is necessary is to tick the rent-a-room box at the beginning of the land and property page of the tax return.

Case Study - 58 : Rent-a-Room Relief (2)

Howard is a bachelor but lives in a luxury five-bedroom detached house on the outskirts of London. He is also a higher-rate taxpayer.

He decides to let a room to a newly graduated doctor for £6,000 per annum.

Howard will have no tax liability on the first £4,250. However, he will be liable to pay tax on the remaining £1,750 of income at 40%. This means that he will be liable to pay £700 in tax.

If you decide to let a room in your main residence and claim the relief, then you must inform the Inland Revenue. This is regardless of whether you will have a tax liability.

If you do not inform the revenue, then you will be taxed as though you are running a normal property-letting business, where your expenses will be deducted from any rental income you receive.

14.2. Choosing Not to Use the Relief

Tax Tip - 16
Consider not using the relief if you have high income and also high expenses.

If you are letting a room in your property, then it is not necessary that you claim the relief. As mentioned in the previous section, you will be taxed as a normal property-letting business if you do not inform the Inland Revenue that you want to use the relief.

Generally speaking, if your rental income is going to be significantly greater than £4,250, then it may not be beneficial to use the relief.

The following two case studies illustrate typical scenarios when it is beneficial to use each method.

Case Study - 59 : When it is Beneficial to Use the Rent-a-Room Relief

John is a higher-rate taxpayer and lets out a room in his property for £7,000 per annum. His expenses are £1,000.

Tax liability if rent-a-room relief is *not* claimed
If rent-a-room relief is not claimed, then he has a taxable income of £6,000 (i.e., £7,000 – £1,000).

This means that his tax liability is calculated as follows:
40% × £6,000 = **£2,400**

Tax liability if rent-a-room relief *is* claimed
If rent-a-room relief is claimed, then he has a taxable income of £2,750 (i.e., £7,000 – £4,250).

This means that his tax liability is calculated as follows:
40% × £2,750 = **£1,100**

As you can see from the above case study, it is beneficial for John to claim the rent-a-room relief. This is because by claiming it, John will pay **£1,300** less in tax on an annual basis. Over a 10-year period, this is **£13,000** in tax savings.

Case Study - 60 : When it is NOT Beneficial to Use the Rent-a-Room Relief

Lisa is a higher-rate taxpayer and lets out a room in her property for £9,000 per annum. Her expenses are £6,000 per annum.

Tax liability if rent-a-room relief is *not* claimed
If rent-a-room relief is not claimed, then she has a taxable income of £3,000 (i.e., £9,000 – £6,000).

This means that her tax liability is calculated as follows:
40% × £3,000 = **£1,200**

Tax liability if rent-a-room relief *is* claimed
If rent-a-room relief is claimed, then she has a taxable income of £4,750 (i.e., £9,000 – £4,250).

This means that her tax liability is calculated as follows:
40% × £4,750 = **£1,900**

As you can see from the above case study, it is beneficial for Lisa *not* to use the rent-a-room relief. This is because by claiming it, Lisa will pay **£700** less in tax on an annual basis. Over a 10-year period, this is **£7,000** in tax savings.

14.3. Renting Out in Joint Ownership

The Inland Revenue states that

> ***'The exemption limit of £4,250 is reduced to £2,125 if during the tax year to April 5, someone else received income from letting accommodation in the same property.'***

This is likely to occur if you own a property in a partnership.

15. Generous Tax Breaks for Holiday Lets

In this section you will become familiar with the tax benefits associated with those who provide holiday lets.

15.1. Qualifying Criteria for a Holiday Let

If you let a property in a popular holiday location, e.g., the south coast, then you could well be operating a holiday lettings business. This is especially the case if your target market is people visiting and staying in your property for short periods of time.

In order to qualify your property as a holiday let, it must be fully furnished; that is, anyone moving into the property must be able to live out of the property without having to buy any additional furniture/furnishings.

It must also satisfy the following three conditions:

- the property must be available to let to the public on a commercial basis for at least 140 days;
- the property must be let for at least 70 days;
- the property must not be occupied by the same individual for more than 31 consecutive days during at least 7 months of the year, which need not be continuous but which includes any months containing any of the 70 let days.

Income tax on a holiday let is charged in the same way as if you are operating a normal lettings business, where tax will be liable on any rental profits less expenses.

Case Study - 61 : Holiday Lets

John buys a three-bedroom property in Bournemouth. His investment strategy is to rent the property in the summer periods to visiting holiday makers.

He offers the property for £250 per week.

Over the financial year, it is let for 35 weeks, which means that he has received a total rental income of £8,750. His expenses are £2,750.

This means that he is liable to pay tax on the £6,000 profit.

15.2. Three Generous Tax Benefits Associated With Holiday Lets

Operating a holiday letting business has three *significant* tax benefits. These are detailed below.

15.2.1. Offsetting losses against other income

If you are unfortunate enough to make a loss in your holiday lettings business, then the loss is treated as a trading loss and can be offset against any other source of income that you have, in the same way as trading losses.

Case Study - 62 : Holiday Lets – Offsetting Losses

Kiran buys a property for the purpose of holiday letting for £130,000 in 1995.

Her first year of letting is very tough and she makes a £2,500 rental loss.

However because she is employed with a salary of £35,000, she is able to offset the loss against this income.

In other words she pays less tax on her employment income.

15.2.2. Re-investment of capital gains

If you decide to sell your holiday let and make a capital gain, then the profit can be re-invested into another qualifying asset, thus avoiding any immediate capital gains tax liability. This therefore means that you will not liable to pay any capital gains tax until you dispose of the asset you have re-invested in.

However, you can continue selling and re-investing the profits. By doing this, you will continue to defer any tax liability until the point at which you stop re-investing the profit.

Case Study - 63 : Holiday Lets – Re-investment of capital gains

Continuing from the previous example.

Kiran sells her property 5 years later for £230,000, thus meaning she has made a profit of £100,000.

She buys another 'holiday let' property in the same tax year by re-investing the profits from the sale and therefore is able to defer any CGT liability.

15.2.3. Business asset taper relief

Because a holiday let property is classed as a business asset, you can claim business asset taper relief. This is more generous relief than non–business asset taper relief.

How to Slash Your Property Capital Gains Tax

16. Understanding Capital Gains Tax (CGT)

Before we look at the different ways to cut your capital gains tax saving strategies, it is important to understand what is meant by the term **capital gains tax (CGT)** and when property investors are liable to pay it.

In this section you will become familiar with CGT and how it is calculated when you decide to sell your property.

16.1. When You Are Liable to Pay CGT

A property investor is likely to incur a CGT liability in the following two situations:

a) when a property is sold at a higher price than for which it was purchased;

b) when a property, or part of a property, is transferred to a non-spouse.

Tax Tip - 17
Properties and other assets can be transferred between husband and wife freely, without triggering a CGT liability.

Both of the above situations are illustrated in the following case studies.

Case Study - 64 : CGT Liability When Selling a Property

Maria purchases a buy-to-let property in January 1998 for £100,000. She rents it out for five years and then sells it for £210,000.

This means that she has made a capital gain of £110,000, upon which she is liable to pay CGT.

Case Study - 65 : CGT Liability When Transferring a Property

Maria purchases a buy-to-let property in January 1998 for £100,000. She rents it out for five years and then gifts the property to her mother.

She receives no payment from her mother for the property.

Although Maria has received no payment for the property, she is treated as having transferred the property to her mother at 'market value,' which is £210,000.

Therefore, again, Maria is liable to pay CGT on the £110,000 profit.

Tax Tip - 18

Property dealers/traders are not liable to pay CGT. When they sell a property, the profit is classed as a dealing profit, and therefore they are liable to pay **income tax** on the profits.

16.2. How Your CGT Bill is Calculated

Calculating the tax liability on the sale or transfer of a property is not easy.

Given the property price increases over the past few years alone, investors are sitting on significant capital gains.

It is important to realise that a number of reliefs and strategies are available to reduce any CGT liability you may have. The most significant of these are detailed in the remainder of this guide.

However, listed in the table below are the typical reliefs/reductions that can be claimed when a property is sold/transferred.

If applicable, these can be offset against the capital gain made on the property and can be used to significantly reduce any tax liability.

Relief/Reduction	Description
Buying and Selling Costs	Typical purchase costs include • solicitor' fees; • mortgage booking fee; • survey costs; • cost of searches, e.g., land, mining, etc. Typical selling costs include • agency fees; • solicitor' fees; • redemption penalties, etc. See section 22.3 for further details.
Capital Costs	If you have made costs of a capital nature, then these can also be offset. A capital cost is one that has increased the price of the property. Examples of capital costs include the building of conservatories, additional bedrooms, loft conversions, garage conversions, etc.

Indexation Relief	This relief was available up until 1998. See section 20.2 for further details.
Private Residence Relief	This relief is based on the period that the property was classed as your PPR. See section for further details.
Private Letting Relief	This relief is a very generous relief that can reduce your capital gain by up to an additional £40,000. See section 18.3 for further details.
Allowable Losses	If you have incurred capital losses, then these can be offset against any capital gain made when you dispose of your property. See section 22.2 for further details.
Taper Relief	This relief was introduced in April 1998 and was a replacement for indexation relief. See section 20.3 for further details.
Personal CGT Allowance	For the 2006–2007 tax year, this allowance is £8,800. See section 22.1 for further details.

17. Avoid CGT by Using 'Private Residence Relief'

In this section you will become familiar with the extremely powerful **private residence relief**.

This allowance on its own can wipe out tens or even hundreds of thousands of pounds of your capital gains tax bill.

17.1. What is Private Residence Relief?

This relief is available to you if you have lived in a property that has been classed as your **main residence** for a period of time.

This relief is not available to you if you are a property dealer and purchased a property with the sole intention of making a dealing profit, i.e., you did not make it your main residence.

The technical name for a person's main residence is **principle private residence (PPR)**.

> **Tax Tip - 19**
> If you have lived in a property that has been your PPR, then you are not liable to pay any capital gains tax on the price appreciation that is attributed to the period when you lived in the property.

There are two types of residence relief that are available, and both are described and illustrated in the following two sections.

17.1.1. Full residence relief

If the property has been classed as your PPR throughout your period of ownership, then you can claim **full residence relief**.

If you can claim full residence relief, then this means that you will have no CGT liability. This is regardless of the capital profit you have made on the property.

Every homeowner who has occupied their property since the first day of ownership up until the time of sale is entitled to use this relief.

> **Case Study - 66 : Full Residence Relief**
>
> Alex buys his first home in May 1990 for £65,000. He lives in it from the day of purchase up until the day he sells it in June 2001. The selling price is £150,000, which means that he has made a capital profit of £85,000.
>
> He is not liable to pay any tax on this profit as he is able to claim full residence relief because the property was his main residence during his period of ownership.

17.1.2. *Partial residence relief*

You are able to claim **partial residence relief** if your property has been your main residence for a period of time but not for the whole period of ownership.

If you are claiming partial residence relief, then the amount of relief you can claim is determined by dividing the periods when the property was classed as your PPR by the total periods of ownership.

For example, if you purchased a property, let it out for 7 years and then lived in it for three years before selling it then you will be able to claim 3/10 partial residence relief. This is because you owned the property for 10 years, but it was your main residence for three of those years.

You are most likely to claim partial residence relief if

- you have a second home (see section 21 for more details on how you can legitimately reduce your tax liability by nominating your main residence);
- you are a property investor who has let a property after having previously lived in it.

17.2. How Long in a Property Before It Can Be Classed as My PPR?

This is one of the most commonly asked tax questions.

The reason for the popularity of this question is because if you can prove that a property was genuinely your PPR, you can make use of some very generous tax reliefs. You will see in the following strategies exactly how you can use these reliefs to your advantage to reduce or even wipe out any tax liability.

The Inland Revenue has not given any specific guidance as to how long you need to live in a property before you can claim that it has been your principle private residence.

However, as a general rule of thumb, you should try to make it your permanent residence for at least one year, i.e., 12 months.

The longer you live in a property, the better chance you have of claiming residence relief.

The Inland Revenue is not necessarily interested in how long you lived in the property. They are *much more* interested in whether the property really was your home and whether you *really* did live in the property!

If you want to claim this relief, here are some pointers that will help you to convince the taxman that a property genuinely was your private residence.

a) Have utility and other bills in your own name at the property address.

   Typical bills will include

   i. gas bills;

ii. water rates;
iii. electricity supply bills;
iv. council tax bills;
v. TV licence, etc.

b) Make the property address your voting address on the electoral register.

c) Be able to demonstrate that you bought furniture and furnishings for the property. Keep receipts and prove that bulky furniture was delivered to the property address.

d) Have all bank statements delivered to the property address.

By following the above guidelines, you will be in a good position to convince the taxman that a property was genuinely your home.

18. The EASIEST Way to Legitimately Avoid CGT

In this section you will learn about two key CGT saving reliefs that are available to property investors.

These two reliefs are known as the

- 36-month rule and
- private letting relief.

18.1. Understanding the '36-Month Rule'

Provided that a house has at some time been your **main residence**, the last three years of ownership are always treated as though you lived there (for the purposes of working out the number of PPR years in the capital gains tax calculation; see section 18).

This is the case even if you didn't actually live there in those last three years.

Tax Tip - 20

Over the last three years, numerous property investors who know about this tax relief have bought new property but retained and let out their existing property.

If you are one of these investors, then if you sell your property now, you will still have no CGT liability!

This is regardless of the significant price increases over the past few years!

The two case studies below show how this rule can be used to provide both Full residence relief and Partial residence relief.

Case Study - 67 : Using the 36-Month Rule to Get Full Residence Relief

Joanne buys an apartment in London docklands in 1990 for £100,000.

She lives in the apartment for eight years before she decides to move in with her long-term boyfriend. She rents her apartment for three years before deciding to sell it.

The apartment is sold in 2001 for £250,000.

Joanne will have no CGT liability on the profit of £150,000 as she is able to claim full residence relief; that is, her entire 11 years of ownership is exempt from CGT. This is because for eight years the property was her PPR and therefore there is no CGT liability on this period of ownership.

Also, she is able to claim the **36-month rule**, which means that the last three years of ownership are also exempt from CGT.

Case Study - 68 : Using the 36-Month Rule to Get Partial Residence Relief

Imagine the same scenario as above, but instead of selling the property in 2001, Joanne decides to let the property for an additional three years. This means that she sells the property in 2004.

The selling price of the property is £325,000, and therefore she realises a capital gain of £225,000.

The amount of partial residence relief that she can claim is calculated as follows.

Total period of ownership = 14 years
Period when property was her PPR = 8 years
Number of years property was let = 6 years

Because the property has been her PPR, she is able to claim three years of additional relief due to the 36-month rule relief.

This means that she is able to claim 11/14 partial residence relief.

Therefore partial residence relief = 11/14 × £225,000 = £176,786.

This means that she will not be liable to pay any CGT on £176,786 of the £225,000 gain due to the principle private residence relief rule.

18.2. How to Use the 36-Month Rule to Your Advantage

If you have invested in property and let it out as soon as you have purchased it, then you can still benefit from using the 36-month rule.

All you need to do is make the property your PPR before you sell it.

You do not need to live in a property before you let it out in order to claim the 36-month rule.

Case Study - 69 : Making a Property Your PPR After It Has Been Let

Bill gets onto the property investment ladder by purchasing a one-bedroom apartment in Manchester in July 1999 for £110,000.

Shortly after purchasing it, he rents it out for the following three years, after which time he considers selling it as it is providing him with a capital gain of £70,000.

Unfortunately, Bill is a higher-rate taxpayer, so he will be liable to pay tax at 40% on the £70,000 profit. This means that he will have a £28,000 tax liability.

Instead, he decides to move into the apartment, making it his PPR, and sells it a year later for £190,000. This means he has made a capital profit of £80,000.

However, he is now able to claim partial residence relief on the property.

The amount of partial residence relief that he can claim is calculated as follows.

Total period of ownership = 4 years
Period when property was his PPR = 1 years
Number of years property was let = 3 years

Because the property has been his PPR, he is able to claim the 36-month rule relief.

This means that he is able to claim 3/4 partial residence relief.

Therefore partial residence relief = 3/4 × £80,000 = £60,000.

This means that assuming no other reliefs are claimed, he will only be liable to pay tax at 40% on the £20,000 profit, which equates to an £8,000 tax liability.

18.3. Wiping Out CGT by Using Private Letting Relief

Tax Tip - 21

If you still have a taxable capital gain after using the 36-month rule, then it is possible that any tax liability can be eliminated by using the **private letting relief**.

The Inland Revenue states that the private letting relief can be used where

- **you sell a dwelling house which is, or has been, your only or main residence, and**
- **part or all of it has at some time in your period of ownership been let as a residential accommodation.**

The amount of private letting relief that can be claimed cannot be greater than £40,000, and it must be the lowest of the following three values:

- £40,000;
- the amount of private residence relief that has already been claimed;
- the amount of any chargeable gain that is made due to the letting; that is, this is the amount that is attributed to the increase in the property value during the period it was let.

The use of this relief is best illustrated via the following case study.

Case Study - 70 : Private Letting Relief

Roger buys a three-bedroom semi-detached house in North Wales for £50,000 in 1990.

He lives in the house for two years and then decides to move to a bigger four-bedroom detached house. He rents out the three-bedroom house for the next five years.

In 1997 he sells the three-bedroom house for £120,000. This means that he has made a capital gain of £70,000.

5/7ths of the profit is exempt from CGT because he is able to claim partial residence relief (two years PPR and the 36-month rule).

This means that he is only liable to pay CGT on the remaining £20,000 of chargeable gain. However, Roger is also able to claim private letting relief, and the amount he can claim is the lower of the following three values:

- £40,000;
- amount of private residence relief already claimed is £50,000;
- amount of any chargeable gain that is made due to the letting is £20,000 (assuming that property increased by £10,000 in each of the two years that the property was let).

This means that Roger is allowed to claim private letting relief of £20,000 as this is the lower of the three values.

Therefore the outstanding chargeable gain of £20,000 is cancelled out by this relief, which means that he has absolutely no CGT liability.

In other words, Roger has made a tax-free capital gain of £70,000 just by having lived in a property for two years!

In this section you have come across two of the most powerful CGT reduction strategies available to property investors—make sure you consider them both before you decide to sell your property!

19. Increasing Property Value and Avoiding Tax

In this section you will become familiar with a tax relief that allows you to claim capital gains relief on the first 12 months of property ownership.

You will also learn how property developers are taking advantage of this relief to grow property portfolios without incurring a CGT liability.

19.1. No CGT on the First 12 Months of Ownership

More and more investors are increasingly facing a situation where they purchase a property but are unable to occupy it immediately due to a variety of legitimate reasons.

- You are having the property built, or
- You are altering or re-decorating the property, or
- You remain in your old home whilst you are selling it.

If you are unable to move into the property immediately after you have purchased it, then it is possible to claim 12 months relief. What this means is that the first 12 months of ownership will still be exempt from any capital gains tax. This is regardless of whether you currently have another property that is your main residence.

However, in order to claim this relief, you *must* occupy the property within 12 months of the purchase.

Case Study - 71 : First 12 Months of Ownership

Asif lives with his family in a two-bedroom terraced house.

In January 1998 he buys a run-down three-bedroom semi-detached property that requires a significant amount of development and modernisation. The property is purchased for £70,000.

The development and modernisation work starts in February 1998 and is completed 10 months later, in December 1998. The total cost of the project is £20,000.

Before he moves into the property with his family, Asif has the property valued at £120,000. This means that the property has appreciated by £30,000 (i.e., 120,000 – (£70,000 + £20,000)).

There will be no tax liability on the gain of £30,000. This is because for the purposes of working out the number of PPR years in the capital gains tax calculation the first year can be treated as though Asif and his family actually lived in the property.

19.2. Using the Rule to Grow a Portfolio Without Paying CGT

Using the **first 12 months of ownership rule** is quite an effective property tax–saving strategy for builders and property developers. This is because they are able to build/develop a property whilst living out of another property. When the new property is ready, they are able to rent out or sell the existing property before moving into the new property.

Case Study - 72 : Exploiting the First 12 Months of Ownership Rule

Alex is a property builder by trade who lives out of his two-bedroom apartment.

He decides to build his own three-bedroom detached house. The house is completed within 12 months of purchasing the land, so he decides to rent out the apartment and move into the new three-bedroom house.

Three years later, he sells the apartment and buys another piece of land, and this time he builds a four-bedroom property. Again, it is built and occupied within 12 months, and again he rents out the existing property.

Alex carries on with this cycle of selling his let property and buying land every four years in order to build a bigger house, which he occupies within 12 months.

On the sale of each property Alex will have no CGT liability. This is because

- the first 12 months will be exempt from tax;
- the time he lives in the property will also be exempt from CGT;
- and the last three years of ownership will also be exempt from CGT.

The tax strategy demonstrated in the above case study illustrates how you can quite effectively grow a portfolio and avoid having a CGT liability. However, as demonstrated in the case study, you would need to be prepared to relocate every four to five years to take advantage of the tax-free gain.

This strategy can be used equally well for property developers who buy run-down properties and then move into them before moving onto the next project.

Be wary of the Inland Revenue!
By using the above strategy, Bill will be able to avoid paying CGT as he is genuinely living in a property for a decent period of time, i.e., 4 years. If you try to adopt such a strategy on a smaller timescale, i.e., where you move more frequently, then the Inland Revenue may well challenge your motive, and you may be liable to pay income tax on the sale of your properties—**so be warned**!

20. Avoid CGT by Maximising Length of Property Ownership

One of the basic buy-to-let property investment principles is to invest for the long term. This is because historically, property investment has always given a healthy return over any long-term period, e.g., 10 years.

The longer you invest in property, the greater tax benefit you will have.

In this section we will look at three further ways of reducing your tax bill.

20.1. Properties Purchased Before 1982

If the property was purchased before March 1982, then you must use an estimate for the value of the property in March 1982 when calculating your CGT liability.

This means that any capital gain arising prior to March 1982 is exempt from CGT.

Case Study - 73 : Properties Purchased Before 1982

Fred buys an investment property in September 1970 for £6,000. He decides to sell it in April 2003 for £125,000.

The estimated value of the property in March 1982 is £20,000.

Therefore this price is used for CGT purposes.

This means that the £14,000 of capital growth that occurred before March 1982 is exempt from any CGT liability.

20.2. Indexation Relief

This is a tax relief that is available for properties that were purchased before 6 April 1998.

The Inland Revenue states that it is

'An allowance that adjusts gains for the effects of inflation up to 1998.'

It is an allowance that equates to the amount a property would have appreciated on a monthly basis if the property value had kept in line with inflation.

Tax Tip - 22
The relief is also available for capital improvements that were made on the property.

The indexation relief is calculated by using the following formulas.

Indexation relief for property

Indexation Relief = Cost of property purchase × Indexation factor

Indexation relief for capital improvement

Indexation Relief = Cost of capital improvement × Indexation factor

The indexation factor is determined by using the table in Appendix A—Indexation Factors for Calculating Indexation Relief.

The following two case studies illustrate the use of indexation relief when purchasing a property and when making a capital improvement.

Case Study - 74 : Indexation Relief on Purchase Price

Mary buys an investment property in June 1985 for £25,000. She sells the property in June 2004 for £75,000.

The indexation relief is calculated as follows.

Cost of property purchase = £25,000
Indexation factor for June 1985 = 0.704

Indexation relief = £25,000 × 0.704

= £17,600

This means that Mary is able to claim £17,600 in indexation relief when she sells her property.

Case Study - 75 : Indexation Relief on Capital Improvement

Following on from the previous case study, Mary makes a capital improvement to her property in September 1990. She builds a conservatory at a cost of £15,000.

The indexation relief on the capital improvement is calculated as follows.

Cost of property purchase = £15,000
Indexation factor for Sept 1990 = 0.258

Indexation relief = £15,000 × 0.258

= £3,870

This means that Mary is able to claim £3,870 in indexation relief when she sells her property.

20.3. Non-business Taper Relief

Non-business taper relief became effective on 6 April 1998. This tapering relief is a replacement for indexation relief, and it is available for non-business-related assets, such as properties.

This means that prior to 6 April 1998, only indexation relief can be claimed, and from 6 April 1998 onward, only taper relief can be claimed.

The amount of relief available is dependant upon the period of property ownership. Taper relief starts once you have owned the property for a minimum of three years and increases to a maximum of 40% of the gain after 10 years.

The table below illustrates how the relief is calculated.

Number of Complete Years Held	% of Gain Chargeable	Effective Tax Rates		
Less than 3 years	100	40	20	10
	100	40	20	10
	100	40	20	10
3	95	38	19	9.5
4	90	36	18	9
5	85	34	17	8.5
6	80	32	16	8
7	75	30	15	7.5
8	70	28	14	7
9	65	26	13	6.5
10 or more years	60	24	12	6

It is important to understand that the relief is only available for complete years of ownership. This means that if the property was owned for 4 years and 11 months, then only 4 years can be claimed.

Tax Tip - 23

Try to make sure that the property is sold after a full year of ownership has been completed. For example, if you have owned a property for 7 years and 11 months, then try to delay the sale for an additional month so that you can claim 8 years of relief.

Case Study - 76 : Non-business Taper Relief

Howard is a higher-rate taxpayer who buys an investment property in June 1998 for £100,000.

The property is let for almost five years and is sold in April 2003 for £200,000.

Howard is able to claim four years non-business taper relief as he has owned the property for four complete years. If he had held onto the property for an additional two months, he would have been able to claim five years relief.

This means that he is liable to pay tax on 90% of the capital gain.

Therefore on the £100,000 capital gain, he will pay tax at 40% on £90,000.

20.4. Bonus Year of Taper Relief

A bonus year of non-business taper relief is available if you purchased a property before 17 March 1998 and sold it after 6 April 1998.

Case Study - 77 : Bonus Year of Taper Relief

Joanne buys an investment property on 1 April 1995 for £65,000 and holds onto it for nine years before deciding to sell it for £165,000 in June 2004.

In this particular scenario, Joanne is able to claim both indexation relief and non-business taper relief.

The amount that can be claimed is as follows.

<u>Indexation relief</u>

Cost of property purchase	= £65,000
Indexation factor for April 1995	= 0.091
Indexation relief	= £65,000 × 0.091
	= **£5,915**

<u>Non-business taper relief</u>
Joanne is able to claim a total of seven years of non-business taper relief. This is because six years can be claimed for the period of ownership from 6 April 1998 to 15 June 2004. Also, the additional bonus year can be claimed because the property was purchased prior to 17 March 1998.

21. Nominating Residence to Avoid CGT

In this section you will understand how people with more than one family home can limit or even avoid CGT on the sale of their second homes.

21.1. Having More Than One Family Home

If you have purchased a second home over the past years, it is extremely likely that you will face a considerable CGT liability when you decide to sell it.

A common scenario for having a second home is if you live in a city/town that is close to your place of work but also own a property where you go to spend your vacations, e.g., on the southeast coast of England.

If you are able to own multiple homes, then you may well save a considerable amount of tax by nominating your residence to the Inland Revenue.

21.2. Nominating Your Residence to the Inland Revenue

If you decide to sell a property, consider nominating it as your main residence to save on tax.

In order to make a nomination you must

a) inform the Inland Revenue in writing which property is your main residence;
b) make the nomination within two years after acquiring the second property.

Tax Tip - 24
REMEMBER: A property cannot be nominated as your main residence if it is let out.

The following case study demonstrates how a potential CGT liability can be wiped out by nominating a different residence.

Case Study - 78 : Switching Residence to Avoid CGT

Bill lives in a two-bedroom apartment in London and works as a stock broker in the heart of the city centre. He purchased his apartment in June 1995.

In June 1999 he also decides to buy a semi-detached three-bedroom house in Southampton that is just by the coast. He starts to spend most of his weekends there with his girlfriend.

In April 2001 Bill realises that his house in Southampton has significantly increased in value and that he will face a considerable CGT liability if he decides to sell.

He takes professional advice and is told to nominate his house in Southampton as his main residence.

He therefore notifies the Inland Revenue in writing that the house in Southampton is his 'nominated' main residence. This is done in June 2001 and means that the house is treated as his main residence from June 1999[6].

Bill decides to sell the house in June 2003 for a £150,000 profit and has no CGT liability. This is because

a) the house is exempt for the first two years because it has been nominated as his main residence;
b) the last two years are exempt due to the 36-month rule (see section 18.2).

Once the house has been sold, Bill notifies the Inland Revenue that his London apartment is now his main residence from June 2001 (i.e., from two years ago). This means that when he sells his apartment in June 2005, 8/10ths of partial residence relief can be claimed.

This is determined as follows.

- Bill has owned the apartment for 10 years.
- Four years partial residence relief is due because between June 1995 and June 1999 it was his classed as his main residence.
- An additional four years partial residence relief is due because between June 2001 and June 2005 it was again classed as his main residence.

This means that by switching and nominating his main residence, Bill has totally avoided any CGT liability on his three-bedroom house and also achieved an additional two years of tax-free capital gain.

[6] A principle private residence election can be backdated to take effect at a date two years before the date of the election

22. Other Ways to Reduce Your CGT Bill

In this section you will learn how you can reduce your CGT liability even further by

- using your annual CGT allowance;
- offsetting previous capital losses;
- timing the sale of your property.

22.1. Using Your Annual CGT Allowance

Each individual has a capital gains tax allowance that can be claimed in the tax year. What this means is that if you have made a capital gain on the sale of an asset, then you can offset the CGT allowance for the tax year in which the asset was sold.

When making a sale with a capital gain, it is important to understand the following two key points:

- if the entire allowance has already been claimed in the tax year, then it cannot be claimed again in the same tax year;

- if part of the allowance has already been claimed in the tax year, then only the outstanding unclaimed amount can be claimed.

The CGT allowances for the current and previous two tax years are detailed in the table below.

	Tax Year		
	2004–2005	**2005–2006**	**2006-2007**
CGT Allowance	£8,200	£8,500	£8,800

The following case study helps to explain how the allowance can be used:

Case Study - 79 : Claiming the Entire Personal CGT Allowance

Bill sells his investment property on 10th April 2006 and has a £9,000 capital gain.

The only tax allowance he is able to claim is his personal CGT allowance, which is £8,800 for 2006–2007, and to date, this has not been claimed.

This means that after this allowance has been deducted from his capital gain (i.e., £9,000 – £8,800) he is liable to pay tax on the remaining gain of £500.

If Bill sells another asset with a capital gain in the 2006–2007 tax year, then he is not able to use his personal CGT allowance again.

This is because the entire CGT allowance for that tax year has already been used.

Case Study - 80 : Claiming Partial Personal CGT Allowance

Fred sells his investment property on 10th April 2004 and has only a £5,000 capital gain.

The only tax relief he is able to claim is his personal CGT allowance, which is £8,200 for 2004–2005.

However, only £5,000 of the allowance needs to be claimed to wipe out the capital gain.

This means that once £5,000 of the allowance has been deducted from his capital gain, he has no CGT.

If Fred sells another asset with a capital gain in the 2004–2005 tax year, he is still able to offset up to £3,200 on any other capital gain arising in the same tax year.

22.2. Capital Losses

If you have made losses on previous 'qualifying' assets, then you can register these losses with the Inland Revenue and offset these against any future capital gains.

Examples of 'qualifying' assets include

- property (e.g., you have a number of residential investment properties);
- shares in a company (e.g., you have shares in LloydsTSB Bank);
- units in a unit trust.

Tax Tip - 25

If you have made any losses, inform the Inland Revenue of the losses in the tax year in which they were incurred. For example, if you made a loss in a share-trading deal in May 2005, then register this with the Inland Revenue in the 2005–2006 tax return.

If you are unable to or you forget to register your losses, you can still claim these losses up to five years after the tax return detailing the losses was due.

This is illustrated in the following case study.

Case Study - 81 : Claiming Partial Personal CGT Allowance

Louise buys £20,000 of shares in Marconi at the height of the technology boom in May 2000. Unfortunately, the share price crumbles, and she ends up selling the shares 12 months later for a total value of £200.

This means that she has made a loss of £19,800.

She is unaware that she can register this loss with the Inland Revenue so that it can be offset against any future capital gain.

Had she known, she would have registered this loss in her 2001–2002 tax return.

After her misfortunes in the stock market, Louise decides to focus on property instead and buys an apartment in Birmingham in June 2001 for £120,000. She decides to sell it in June 2004 for £170,000. This gives her a capital gain of £50,000.

She takes tax advice and is told by her advisor that she is still able to register her losses with the Inland Revenue. In fact, as long as she registers the losses with the Inland Revenue by January 2008, they can be offset against any future capital gain.

This means that she can reduce her taxable gain on the sale of the property by £19,800 immediately.

If you have made any losses on qualifying assets, then make sure that they are registered with the Inland Revenue!

22.3. Buying and Selling Costs

What many property investors fail to realise is that if you have incurred costs when buying and selling your property, then these can also be offset when the property is sold.

Typical buying costs will include

- solicitors fees;
- surveyor costs;
- land registry fees;
- solicitor's indemnity insurance;
- local authority searches, etc.

Typical selling costs will include

- solicitors fees;
- estate agency fees;
- advertising costs;
- accountancy fees, etc.

22.4. Selling at the Right Time Can Save You Tax!

The time when you decide to sell a property can have a significant bearing on how much tax you will save.

Before you sell your property, make sure you consider the following key pointers.

a) <u>Full year's taper relief</u>

As mentioned in section 20.4, if you are close to a complete year of property ownership (three years or more), then try to hold out for the additional months required to complete the year.

If you do this, then you will benefit from an additional year's taper relief.

b) Beginning/end of tax year

If you expect to dispose of a number of capital assets in the same year, then try to sell them in different years to make use of your annual CGT allowance.

With just some simple tax planning you can phase the selling of assets to make sure that you always utilise your CGT allowance.

In particular, try to make sure you use up your annual CGT allowance before the end of the tax year. This is especially the case if you intend to sell multiple assets.

Case Study - 82 : Timing the Sale of Your Property

John owns two buy-to-let properties, and in January 2004 he decides to sell them both so he can reinvest the money into a different area. John believes that he can achieve better returns by investing into an area of major regeneration.

He puts both properties on the market, and a sale is agreed on both of them.

John agrees with the vendors that the sale of one property will be completed in the 2003–2004 tax year so that he can use the CGT allowance of £7,900 for that year.

He also agrees that the second property will be completed in the second week of April 2004, again so that he can use the CGT allowance of £8,200 for the 2004–2005 tax year.

If John had sold the properties in the same tax year, then he would only have been able to use the CGT allowance on the sale of one of the properties.

23. Beware of the Capital Gains Tax Trap

Given the property boom over recent years, a huge number of investors have quickly and successfully grown portfolios by using a very simple investment strategy. This strategy involves withdrawing equity from an existing property to fund the next purchase.

Though this strategy has been successfully used to quickly grow portfolios and increase the number of millionaires in the country, it is has already caused and continues to cause severe CGT implications for a growing number of investors.

Below is a story about a woman called Aleesha –The multi-millionaire property investor who couldn't afford to sell a property. This article was written jointly by Daniel Feingold (BScHons, Barrister-at-Law (NP) International Tax & Law Specialist) and Amer Siddiq.

23.1. Starting to Grow the Portfolio

Case Study - 83 : Aleesha takes her first steps on the property investment ladder

Aleesha buys her first two-bed terraced investment property in January 1996 for £60,000.

This is funded by a £12,000 deposit and a £48,000 buy-to-let mortgage. In January 2000, the property is valued at £100,000, so she decides to fund her next investment property by releasing equity from the existing one.

Her mortgage lender allows her to increase her mortgage borrowing to £80,000 (i.e. 80% of the property value) and therefore she is able to buy a £150,000 three bedroom detached property with the 20% deposit funded by the equity release.

Now there is one very important point to note about the above case study. This is that there is no capital gains tax (CGT) liability due when the property is remortgaged. CGT is only due when the property is sold or transferred. So what this effectively means is that Aleesha is able to extract large sums of money from her property without paying a single penny in tax. In fact, even if she had used the equity release proceeds for a cruise around the world then still no CGT liability would have been triggered.

However, this is a very risky strategy as we are about to realise.

23.2. Remortgaging to Continue the Portfolio the Growth

Case Study - 84 : Aleesha continues her portfolio growth

In 2002, Aleesha's first property is worth £150,000 and the second property is worth £200,000. Again she decides to grow her property portfolio and remortgages the existing properties. She again releases equity to fund FIVE new apartment purchases at £125,000 in the North of England.

Due to the competitive buy-to-let market she is now able to remortgage the properties to 85% of the property value. This means that on her first property she is able to increase her borrowing to £127,500 – more than twice what she originally purchased the property for.

So Aleesha now has FIVE properties with a market value of £125,000, one at £150,000 and another at £200,000. Her total portfolio is worth £975,000 – almost a property millionaire!

23.3. The Property Millionaire

Case Study - 85 : Aleesha becomes a property millionaire

By 2004, the north has had two years of excellent property capital growth and the apartments purchased at £125,000 are now worth £175,000 each, her two bed terraced property is now valued at £175,000 and three bed detached property is valued at £250,000.

She is now a property millionaire!

Again, Aleesha is keen to continue the growth of her property portfolio and once again takes advantage of the 85% equity release available and remortgages all the properties to 85% loan to value and invests in three Villas one in each of Spain, France and Cyprus for £250,000 each.

So to summarise this is the current state of Aleesha's property portfolio:

- Two bed terraced property: Purchased for £60,000. Current value of £175,000 with outstanding mortgage of £148,750
- Three bed detached property: Purchased for £150,000. Current value of £250,000 with outstanding mortgage of £212,500
- FIVE Apartments: Purchased for £125,000 each. Current value of £175,000 each with an outstanding mortgage of £148,750.
- THREE villas in non-UK countries valued at a total of £750,000.

So in total here portfolio is now worth over £2million and she has become a multi-millionaire.

23.4. The Multi-Millionaire Who Can't Afford to Sell a Property

Aleesha, has grown a very sizeable portfolio in a few years and has indeed become a property millionaire (well on paper anyway!).

However, she has never considered her capital gains tax position during her continued investment, and this means that on each of her UK owned properties she actually now owes more than what she originally paid for the property.

This in turn means that unless she has a considerable amount of savings she is unlikely to be able to pay the CGT bill on the sale of the property from the actual sales proceeds.

Lets take the example of her very first investment property, which she purchased in 1996 for £60,000. If she sells at the current market value of £175,000 then she has made a £115,000 capital gain (minus her annual CGT exemption of £8,200) and could be liable to pay tax of 40% (i.e. £42,720) of this amount (ignoring the deductions for indexation and taper relief and costs).

However, given that she only has £26,500 of equity in the property she will be required to find an extra £16,220 just to pay the taxman, thus meaning she has made no actual profit and could incur additional debt paying the taxman. She may think that she can sell another of her properties to fund the required £16,220, but again she will face the same problem, where the sale of the property will not cover its own CGT liability.

Now, if for some reason she needed to sell all her properties then you could see how she could end up paying the taxman quite a considerable amount of money, and have nothing to show for it herself at the end of it.

So, although Aleesha is a millionaire property investor, she could end up without a penny to her name and with significant debts if she decides to sell.

Her foreign properties do not help her either, as there is local CGT (often a compulsory withholding of a percentage of the sale proceeds) and the balance due to the taxman here after deducting the foreign tax she has had to pay.

23.5. How to avoid and overcome the 'Capital Gains Tax Trap Problem'

There are a number of ways to tackle this tax problem and these are outlined below by Daniel Feingold:

23.5.1. Hold the properties and don't sell

Firstly, she could decide not to purchase anymore properties and continue to just hold the properties and wait till they have increased in value, or if purchased with repayment mortgages, enough of the loans have been repaid;

that the sales proceeds could cover any tax liability quite comfortably. However this may take 5, 10, or 20 more years!

One tax advantage of waiting is that after 10 years of ownership of each property; by virtue of taper relief the CGT rate will reduce from 40% to 24%.

23.5.2. Emigrate

Secondly, she could leave the UK for 5 complete tax years and then sell the properties in either the tax year following her year of departure and any of the next 4 tax years. By doing this she would wipe-out any UK CGT liability.

Given that six million UK residents are expected to emigrate by the year 2020 this could be her chosen option. Also, she may quite fancy living in one of her foreign properties. She would also have to consider local CGT in her new Country of residence, on her UK property sales. This would be 15% in Spain. In France, she would at present have no CGT on her UK properties (this may change!) and in Cyprus she would have to pay 20%.

23.5.3. Transferring to a company

Thirdly, she could avoid CGT, if her properties taken together were considered to be a "Business".

She could then transfer them into a Company and claim Incorporation Relief. This would have the effect of enabling the Company to sell the properties with little or no CGT liability.

To find out more about the second and third strategies and how you can overcome the property capital gains tax trap please go to the consultancy section at: http://www.property-tax-portal.co.uk.

24. Using Property Partnerships to Cut Your CGT bill

In section 43 you saw how it was possible to set up property partnerships and how they could be effectively used to reduce your income tax liability.

In this section you will learn how property partnerships can also be used to minimise your capital gains tax liability.

24.1. Making Use of Multiple CGT Allowances

One of the biggest tax benefits of a property partnership is that each person in the partnership can use his/her annual personal CGT allowance when the property is sold.

Case Study - 86 : Using Property Partnerships to Save CGT (1)

Mr. and Mrs. Jamieson purchased a three-bedroom detached house in March 1999 for £175,000.

They decide to sell the property in May 2004 for £300,000.

They have not used the annual CGT allowance for the year, so they are able to each claim their annual allowance of £8,200.

It does not matter how many partners there are as each partner will be allowed to use his/her personal CGT allowance, as long as it has not been used up on the sale of another qualifying asset.

24.2. Save Tax by Transferring to Your Husband/Wife or Civil Partner

In the previous section, it became evident that if you transfer/gift an asset, CGT may be due on any gain made at the time of transfer.

In this section you will become familiar with methods for transferring property between husband and wife to reduce tax.

Tax Tip - 26

DON'T FORGET: Property ownership can be transferred freely between husband and wife.

24.2.1. Transferring to Lower-Rate Taxpayer

If your spouse is a lower-rate taxpayer, then consider moving a greater share of the property ownership into his/her name before the property is sold.

This is especially the case if you are a higher-rate taxpayer and your spouse has minimal income.

24.2.2. Transferring If Spouse or Civil Partner Has Registered Losses

In section 22.2 you learned that if you registered any capital losses, then you could offset any future capital gain on your property against these losses.

However, if your spouse has made losses in his/her sole name, then you can transfer part or the entire property into his/her name to offset the losses against the gain.

Case Study - 87 : Transferring When a Spouse Has Registered Losses

Mr. and Mrs. Karim bought a three-bedroom detached house in 2001 for £150,000 on a buy-to-let basis. Both are higher-rate taxpayers.

Prior to the purchase, Mr. Karim had actively and unsuccessfully traded on the stock market and had run up losses of £50,000. He had registered the losses with the Inland Revenue.

In 2003 they decide to sell the property and invest in the northwest, where they feel they can achieve a better rental income and also higher capital growth.

They decide to sell the property, and it sells for £207,000, thus giving them a capital gain of £57,000.

Prior to the sale the property is moved into the sole name of Mr. Karim. By doing this, they have both successfully avoided any CGT liability.

This is because

a) Mr. Karim can offset the £50,000 of losses that he accumulated through his share dealings;
b) the remaining amount of £7,000 is consumed by his personal CGT allowance for 2003–2004.

If Mr. and Mrs. Karim had continued to own the property as a 50:50 split, they would have had a higher tax liability. This is because they would have both been liable to pay tax on £20,600 each (after the personal CGT allowance for 2003–2004 had been deducted).

Therefore their tax liabilities would have been as follows:

Mr Karim:	0.4 × £20,600	=	£8,240
Mrs Karim:	0.4 × £20,600	=	£8,240
	Combined Tax Liability:		**£16,480**

As you can see, by transferring property in this way, they have made huge tax savings of £16,480.

Tax Tip - 27
If you are one of the thousands of people who have lost money on the stock market, then consider selling your loss-making stocks/shares before you sell a property with a significant capital gain.

24.3. Transferring Strategies for Non-spouse and Non-civil Partnerships

In this section you will become familiar with important considerations you need to make before transferring to a non-spouse.

24.3.1. Transferring in Stages

A good tax planning strategy for avoiding or minimising CGT is to transfer the property ownership in stages.

If you do this, then you can use your annual CGT allowance over a number of years to avoid CGT.

Case Study - 88 : Transferring in Stages

Mr. and Mrs. Higginbottom purchased an investment property for £40,000 in 1998. They are both higher-rate taxpayers.

Their long-term intention is to give the property to their son to help him get onto the property ladder. At the time of purchase they appreciate that they may well have to pay CGT on the transfer at a later date if the property price has increased.

So, they decide to start transferring ownership by using up their annual CGT allowance.

From 1999–2002 they transfer accumulated property capital gain on the property to their son using their combined annual CGT allowance.

By transferring the property in stages and using their annual CGT allowances, they have successfully avoided paying CGT on the property.

DON'T FORGET: Each individual is entitled to use the annual CGT allowance to legitimately reduce their CGT bill. Don't let the allowance go to waste, especially if you know to whom you will be transferring property ownership in the future.

24.4. Transferring at 'Arm's Length'

It is important to understand that whenever a property is transferred or sold to a 'connected person,' the estimated market value at the time of sale/transfer must be used when calculating the CGT liability, instead of the amount paid.

This is because transactions between such people are automatically treated as not being at arm's length.

Connected persons are defined as

- business partners;
- mother, father, or more remote ancestor;
- daughter, son, or more remote descendant;
- brothers and/or sisters;
- those who are regarded as close family by marriage, i.e., in-laws.

Case Study - 89 : Sale Not at Arm's Length

Rebecca buys a property in 1980 for £75,000. Its market value in January 2003 is £350,000.

She decides to sell the property to her younger sister, Aleesha, at a significantly reduced price of £200,000.

It is clear that the transaction is between connected persons and therefore is treated as not having been made at arm's length.

Therefore Rebecca will be taxed as though she has received £350,000 from the sale of the property.

25. Advanced Strategies for Avoiding CGT

This strategy outlines a number of additional reliefs that are available, which can help to reduce the CGT liability further in certain scenarios.

25.1. How to Claim an Additional Three Years of PPR

If you live in a property and then vacate it but return to live in the property again, you can claim up to three years relief. This is known as the **three years' absence relief**.

It is not necessary for the property to have been rented out during the period that it was vacated.

However, for the three years absence relief (sandwiched between periods of actual residence) it does matter if another property was your PPR during those three years, i.e. both properties cannot be your PPR at the same time.

Case Study - 90 : Claiming Additional Three Years' Absence Relief

John buys a two-bedroom property in Manchester in 1985 for £45,000 and lives in it for 10 years.

He then rents a two-bedroom house in London in 1995. He decides to rent out the house in Manchester.

He moves back to Manchester in 1998 (after three years). For the period 1995-1998, John informs the Inland Revenue that the Manchester house was his elected main residence, since he was renting in London

When John moves back to Manchester he lives there for an additional three years and then sells the property in 2001 for £250,000.

This means that the property ownership can be summarised as follows:

- 1985 to 1995 he lived in the property
- 1995 to 1998 he rented the property
- 1998 to 2001 he returned to live in the property again

This means that John has no CGT liability when he sells the property.

This is because for thirteen years the property was his main residence. Also, he is able to claim the three years absence relief when the property was rented out.

Therefore John has made a £205,000 tax-free capital profit!

25.2. Claiming PPR When Working Overseas

If you lived in a property and your employer required you to work overseas, then the period that you spent working overseas can also be claimed as residential relief. This relief can be claimed if you return to the same property and make it your **main residence again**. The time that you spent working overseas is irrelevant.

However, you can only claim this relief if no other residence qualifies for relief during the absence, i.e., you had no other nominated PPR.

Case Study - 91 : Claiming PPR When Working Overseas

Alex buys a two-bedroom house in 1990 for £130,000.

He works as an IT consultant, and in 1992 he is asked to work on a three-year project in the United States. He jumps at the opportunity and decides to let his property whilst working overseas. His work permit is extended and he returns to live in the house in 1999, after seven years.

For the period 1992-1999, Alex informs the Inland Revenue that the two-bedroom house was his elected main residence.

In 2003 he is offered a permanent position in the United States, which he accepts, so he decides to sell his UK property. He has it valued at £300,000.

Alex will have no CGT liability because:

- between 1990 and 1992 he lived in the property, so there is no CGT liability;
- between 1992 and 1999 he could still claim residence relief as he was working outside the country;
- between 1999 and 2003 the property was again his main residence.

Tax Tip - 29

If Alex had bought a property in the United States but not elected to make it his PPR, then he could still claim relief on the UK property under both overseas employment relief and the last three years' ownership relief. If he had elected to make the US property his PPR, then only the last three years' ownership rule would still be effective on his UK property.

25.3. Claiming PPR When Re-locating in the UK

If you live in a property and then your employer requires you to work elsewhere in the UK, then you can claim up to four years' relief. You must return to the property and make it your main residence again.

However, you can only claim this relief if no other residence qualifies for relief during the absence, i.e., you had no other nominated PPR.

Case Study - 92 : Claiming PPR When Re-locating in the UK

John works as an IT consultant. As part of his employment contract, he works at different customer locations throughout the country.

He lives in North Wales, in a house he purchased in 1995 for £60,000. However, he is assigned to a long-term project in London in 1999.

His company provides him with rented accommodation in London, so he decides to live there for the duration of the project.

Because he will be vacating his house in North Wales, he decides to rent it out for an annual rental income of £5,000. He is liable to pay income tax on his rental profits.

John finishes his assignment in London and returns to his house in North Wales in January 2003. For the period 1999-2003, John informs the Inland Revenue that the two-bedroom house was his elected main residence.

After returning to North Wales he lives in his house for a year but then decides to move back to London on a more permanent basis.

His house is valued at £160,000 in February 2004.

John will have no CGT liability because

- between 1995 and 1998 he lived in the property, so there is no CGT liability;
- between 1999 and 2003 the duties of UK employment required him to live elsewhere and there was no other property that was his PPR;
- from January 2003 to February 2004 he lived in the property, so there is no CGT liability.

25.4. CGT Implications of Providing Property to Dependent Relatives

There is no principal private residence relief available to an owner if he doesn't live in the property but his relatives do.

However, if someone owned a property on 5 April 1988 that has been continuously occupied rent-free by a dependant relative since that date, the property is exempt from CGT when the owner disposes of it.

Dependant relative is defined as the owner's own or the owner's spouse's widowed mother or any other relative unable to look after themselves because of old age or infirmity.

There is another possibly tax effective way of providing a home for a relative: by acquiring a property, putting it into trust, and allowing the relative to live in it rent-free for life. However, this is a simplification of the subject, and professional advice must be sought.

Inheritance Tax (IHT) Planning

26. Understanding Inheritance Tax

Inheritance tax is becoming more and more of a 'tax bombshell.'

This is purely because property prices have increased so much over the past few years. If you do not plan for IHT now, then you could be passing on a huge tax liability as well as unwanted stress to your loved ones!

In this section you will become familiar with IHT and what you can do to minimise any future liability.

26.1. What is Inheritance Tax?

Inheritance tax is commonly referred to as a 'gift tax' or 'death tax.'

If at the time of your death you pass on part or the whole of your estate, then the inheritor could be liable to pay inheritance tax.

There is currently an IHT threshold level of £285,000 for the 2006–2007 tax year. Anything above this amount is taxed at 40%, i.e., at the highest rate.

This means that if at the time of death your whole estate is valued at less than £285,000, the inheritor will have no tax to pay.

If the value of the estate is over this amount, then anything above the £285,000 will be taxed at 40%.

Please use the following link to view the IHT rates for previous years:

http://www.hmrc.gov.uk/rates/inheritance.htm

Case Study - 93 : No IHT Liability

At the time of his death, John has an estate that is worth £240,000. His estate is made up of his house, which is worth £200,000, and the £40,000 cash in his savings account.

He gifts his entire estate to his son.

His son will have no IHT liability as it is below the threshold level.

Now, given the dramatic property price increases over the past few years, this threshold level seems to be *very low*.

If parents living in London, and the southeast in particular, were to pass away today, then it is highly likely that they would trigger an immediate tax liability on their loved ones.

This is because a very large number of properties in these areas are already valued at above the IHT threshold level!

The average property price in the United Kingdom in 2020 is predicted to be in excess of £330,000.

This means that more and more people are going to be subject to this tax liability in the future, especially if the last budget is anything to go by, as the threshold level only increased from £275,000 to £285,000!

26.2. One VERY Important Point to Note!

If you die tomorrow and leave the estate to your children, then any IHT liability is due immediately by them.

Case Study - 94 : IHT Due at Time of Death

Death befalls both Albert and his wife.

When Albert died, he left everything to his wife.

When his wife died, she left everything to her son.

At her time of death the estate is valued at £385,000. The son must pay £40,000 in taxes before he can take ownership of the estate.

This is because he is liable to pay tax at 40% on the £100,000 value of the estate that is above the £285,000 threshold level.

Now, in the above case study, if the estate was made up entirely from the value of the property, in which the son lived, then it may well be the case that the property will need to be sold in order to pay the tax liability!

Not only is there a significant tax burden, but there is also a huge inconvenience for the son.

26.3. FOUR Simple Ways to Reduce Inheritance Tax

Tax Tip - 28

There is no IHT liability if a spouse inherits assets from their partner. This is regardless of the value of the inheritance.

Here are four common ways of reducing inheritance tax.

a) Utilising the £285,000 threshold level

   If circumstances are such that your estate is not worth more than the current threshold level, then as mentioned earlier, there is no tax liability for the inheritor.

However, as we have seen earlier in this section, this scenario is becoming more and more unlikely!

b) Gifting to spouse
All gifts between husband and wife are exempt from tax as long as they are both domiciled in the UK.

This means that even if a husband has an estate valued at £10 million pounds, then he can gift this to his wife.

It does not matter if it was gifted during his lifetime or at the time of his death; either way, his wife will incur no tax liability.

c) Gifting as soon as possible during your lifetime
During your lifetime, it can be tax beneficial to gift sooner rather than later. This is especially the case if you know who will inherit your estate.

If you gift during your lifetime, then your inheritor will be in possession of a potentially exempt transfer (PET).

A PET is a lifetime gift to an individual or certain trusts (but not to a company or a discretionary trust). If someone makes PETs amounting to any figure, then there is no lifetime IHT to pay, and if they survive for seven years after the last of those PETs, then there is no IHT to pay on death either.

Tax Tip - 29
The longer you live, the less tax your inheritors will have to pay.

This is because there is a scaling taper relief that is available, which reduces the amount of tax that is liable.

So, if you transfer a property or gift it away and survive for seven years, then the inheritor will have no IHT liability.

The table below shows the how the IHT liability is reduced.

Years Between the Gift/Transfer and Death	% of IHT Charged
0 to 3 years	100%
3 to 4 years	80%
4 to 5 years	60%
5 to 6 years	40%
6 to 7 years	20%
7 years and over	0%

d) Trusts

You have already learned that husband and wife incur no IHT liability when gifting to each other.

However, if you want to gift to your children/relatives, then setting up a trust may be the best option.

Trusts can be used to hold properties as well as other appreciating assets such as stocks and shares.

Properties can be placed into trusts in a tax efficient manner, which can help to significantly reduce and even avoid capital gains or inheritance tax.

There are a number of different types of trusts that can be set up to make tax savings, and each have their own merits and are suitable for different scenarios.

It is strongly recommended if you are considering transferring to your children or other members of your family that you take tax advice from a tax expert.

26.4. Don't Forget Your Capital Gains Liability

Tax Tip - 30

Your capital gains tax liability is not eliminated if you decide to gift/transfer a property.

If you decide to gift/transfer a property, then you are still liable to pay capital gains tax on any profit that *you* have made.

Timing of the transfer is crucial, and if you are not careful when you gift/transfer, then you might be hit with a CGT bill and your inheritor hit with an IHT bill.

Case Study - 95 : Double Tax Liability

Alicia bought an investment property in April 1990 for £125,000, and in June 2004, it is worth £485,000.

She decides to gift the property to her son and leave the country.

However, she soon changes her mind when it becomes evident that her son could be liable to pay IHT up to the amount of £80,000 (£485,000-££285,000 * 40%) and that she will also have a significant tax liability on the £360,000 capital gain.

Instead, she takes tax advice on how to best limit her liabilities.

26.5. How to Avoid Inheritance Tax on Your Family Home

The following article written by James Bailey explains how to successfully avoid Inheritance Tax on your family home.

For most people, the family home is their most valuable asset. Unfortunately, it is also often the asset that admits them to what was once a very exclusive club – the Inheritance Tax club.

Inheritance Tax ("IHT") is charged on a person's "estate" (broadly, assets less liabilities) when they die. The first £285,000 is free of charge (the "nil rate band") and all the rest is charged at 40%. The nil rate band will rise to £325,000 in 2009-10.

Because the nil rate band has not kept pace with house prices, more and more people find themselves in line for what used to be a tax on the rich. Transfers between married couples (or civil partners) are exempt from IHT, so if the home is left to the surviving spouse there is no IHT cost on the first death, but when the survivor dies, the house may well have to be sold to pay the IHT.

Much ingenuity has therefore gone into schemes to avoid IHT on the family home, and these have been countered with much legislation. There was a time when the ageing parent could simply "put the house in the children's names" and continue to live there – this has not been effective for many years, though sadly I still come across situations where people have thought it was, and get an unpleasant surprise when the parent dies and is still taxed on the value of the house.

The three biggest obstacles to IHT planning for the family home are:

- **"Reservation of benefit"** – If you give the house away, but carry on living there, you will be treated as if you still owned it for IHT purposes
- **"Life interests"** – If you do not own the property, but have the right to live there for the rest of your life, you are treated as if you owned it for IHT purposes
- **"Pre-owned Assets Tax"** – This is an annual charge to income tax on the "benefit" of using assets that you once owned in the past, or assets that you

have never owned but which were bought by their owners with money that you gave them.

The tax on pre-owned assets began in 2005, but it catches arrangements made as long ago as 1986. Any future IHT planning might be similarly attacked with retrospective effect, so this is not a planning area for the faint-hearted!

Any IHT planning involving the family home needs expert advice, both to ensure that it works for tax purposes, and also that other vital factors are considered:

- Security for the person living in the house – some schemes rely on the generosity of the children in letting the parent occupy "their" house, but what happens if the children go bankrupt?
- The ability to move house in the future
- The potential problems if nursing home care becomes necessary (the rules on "deliberate deprivation" can deny local authority funding to those who have given assets away)

There are two sorts of planning to consider – lifetime planning, and "first death" planning.

26.5.1. Lifetime planning

The scope here is very limited – but the following can be considered:

- **Give away the home, then pay a full market rent to live there** - but the rent will be taxable income for the new owners of the home
- **Give a share in the home to (say) a child, who then lives there with you and shares the running costs** – but if the child moves out, the value of their share will be included in your estate again
- **Give cash to the children, wait seven years, then sell the house and move into one they buy with the cash** – this works, but only if you have that kind of cash available in the first place
- **Mortgage the house, and invest the money in assets that do not attract IHT, such as shares in unlisted trading companies (perhaps the children run such a company?), or agricultural land which is let out** – after two years, the investments described will qualify for 100% relief from IHT, and the mortgage will reduce the value of the house for IHT purposes – but you have to pay the mortgage interest. I have seen this work, but only because the parent concerned wanted to invest in the children's company anyway.

26.5.2. "First death" planning

If you are a married couple (or a civil partnership), there is some opportunity to pass the home down to the children when the first of you dies – a dead person cannot "reserve a benefit".

The first essential step is to ensure that you own the home as "tenants in common" rather than as "joint tenants". This is because a joint tenant inherits the other joint tenant's share automatically on their death, whereas a tenant in common can leave their share to whomever they wish. If you are joint tenants, it is a simple legal procedure to convert to being tenants in common.

Some planning possibilities on the first death are:

- **Leave your share of the house to the children** – this is the "low-tech" form of planning, and crucially, it relies on the children's generosity in allowing the surviving partner to live there undisturbed (they cannot evict him/her, but they could put a tenant in or force a sale of the property), and on them not going bankrupt. If the survivor wants to sell up and move, there will be capital gains tax to pay on the sale of the house.

- **Leave your share of the house to a "discretionary trust" with your partner and your children as beneficiaries** – assuming that your half of the property is worth less than the "nil rate band" there is no IHT to pay, and when your partner dies they can leave their share to the children as well. If, however, your partner wants to move, there may be CGT to pay when the house is sold, and there is a danger that the Revenue will say that your partner has a "life interest" in the other half of the house. A more sophisticated scheme is:

- **Leave a cash legacy equal to the "nil rate band" to a discretionary trust, and empower that trust to take an index-linked charge over the house instead of cash** – this needs careful drafting to ensure that your partner does not have a "life interest" as before, and it is essential that the trustees of the trust know how to manage things to avoid this problem. The main advantage of this arrangement is that if the survivor wants to move house, they can do so without any CGT being payable on the sale of the old property.

  It may be possible to deal with this planning after the first death, by using a "deed of variation" within two years of the death. This effectively rewrites the will, providing that the beneficiaries agree.

  IHT planning is a complicated business, and it is **essential** to get proper professional help. I will leave you with two pieces of advice:

- **MAKE A WILL**

- **If someone tells you they know a "simple" way to avoid IHT, they do not understand how IHT works!**

26.6. Other IHT Exemptions

26.6.1. Completely Exempt

- Transfers between husband and wife; any transfers that take place between a husband and wife during lifetime and death are exempt from IHT.

- Gifts in consideration of marriage; it is possible for a parent to pay up to £5,000 to their child. The amounts that can be gifted by relatives and other friends are lower.

- Gifts to charities.

- Gifts for national purposes.

- Gifts to political parties.

26.6.2.Annual Exemptions

- It is possible to gift up to £3,000 in any tax year.

- Certain trusts are also exempt from IHT.

Tax Strategies for Commercial Property Investors

27. Tax Liability for Commercial Property Owners

If you are investing in commercial property, then you will be liable to pay the following taxes.

- Income tax (IT)
- Corporation tax (CT)
- Capital gains tax (CGT)
- Inheritance tax (IHT)
- Stamp duty land tax (SDLT)
- Value-added tax (VAT)

27.1. Three Ways to Slash your Commercial Property Tax Bill

a) A commercial property let to an unquoted qualifying trading company is eligible for **business asset taper relief (BATR)**, which reduces the chargeable gain on a property by 50% after one year of ownership and by 75% after two years.

From 6 April 2004, this also applied to a commercial property let to a trading business run by an individual or by a partnership.

b) Owners of industrial buildings are eligible for an **industrial buildings allowance (IBA)**, which is a capital allowance for the first 25 years of the life of the building.

27.2. 100% Capital Allowances for Flats Over Shops

If you decide to renovate or convert vacant/under-used space above shops and other commercial property to provide flats, then you can claim up-front tax relief on the entire capital spending.

The capital allowance that is available for such projects is part of a package offered by the government to help the regeneration of the UK.

27.2.1. Qualifying Properties

If you decide to renovate or convert existing buildings, in order to qualify for this relief, the property must satisfy the following criteria:

a) the commercial property must have been built before 1980;

b) the property must not consist of more than five floors in total;

c) the ground floor of the property can originally have been used as either commercial, residential, or mixed use—however, when the work starts, the entire (or majority part) of the ground floor must be classed as commercial use;

d) all floors above the ground floor must either have been unoccupied or used as storage space for at least one year before the renovation or conversion work starts.

If you decide to convert space into new flats, then the following conditions must be satisfied:

a) the conversion must take place within the boundaries of the existing building—extensions to the original building are only allowed if they are required to provide access;

b) each flat must not have more than four rooms—this excludes the kitchen/bathroom and other small areas such as cloakrooms and hallways;

c) each flat must be self-contained and have its own entry/exit access—the point of entry/exit must be separate to that of the ground floor.

Quoted below is an example from Tolleys Capital Allowances 2002-3, section 5.12.

Case Study - 96 : Claiming Tax Relief When Investing in an EZT

Frances is a travel agent in Brighton operating from the ground floor of a building of which she is the freeholder. The building was constructed in 1960 and has two storeys above the ground floor, which were originally used as a dwelling but which have been empty since 1995.

In the year ending 5 April 2002, Frances incurs capital expenditure of £15,000 in converting the second storey into a flat for the purpose of short-term letting as a dwelling. The flat has three rooms, plus kitchen and bathroom.

Included in the expenditure is £5,000 for an extension to the building, which is required to provide access to the flat. Frances claims a reduced flat conversion initial allowance of 50% of the expenditure for 2001–2002.

The flat is completed and suitable for letting on 1 May 2002. It is let to a person who is not connected with Frances on 1 June 2002 under a three-year lease for £200 a week. In March 2004,

Frances sells the freehold of the building for £250,000. Of the net sale proceeds, £18,000 is attributable to assets representing the conversion expenditure.

Frances' allowances are as follows:

Residue of expenditure	£
2001–2002 qualifying expenditure	15,000
Initial allowance (maximum 100%)	7,500 (7,500)
2002–2003 writing-down allowance (25% of £15,000)	3,750 (3,750)

	3,750
2003–2004 writing-down allowance	
Sale proceeds	(18,000)
Excess of sale proceeds over residue of expenditure	14,250
Balancing charge (restricted to allowances made, 7,500 +	3,750)
	£11,250

Notes

(a) No writing-down allowance is available for 2001–2002 as the flat is not suitable for letting as a dwelling on 5 April 2002 and is therefore not a qualifying flat at that time. It becomes a qualifying flat on 1 May 2002 so that a writing-down allowance is available for 2002–2003. Frances does not hold the relevant interest in the flat on 5 April 2004, having sold the building in March 2004, so no writing-down allowance is available for 2003–2004.

(b) Expenditure on the extension of a building is not a qualifying expenditure, except to the extent that it is required for the purpose of providing a means of entry to the flat (see above).

(c) Assuming that Frances is not otherwise carrying on a Schedule A business, the initial allowance of £7,500 will create a loss for 2001–2002 in the Schedule A business. Frances may claim to set off that loss (which consists entirely of capital allowances) against other income of 2001–2002 or 2002–2003 or may carry it forward against future rental income.

28. Enterprise Zone Trust (EZT)

28.1. What is an Enterprise Zone Trust?

Certain areas in which the government particularly wants to encourage investment have been designated as enterprise zones.

Investors who invest in new (or within two years of first use) commercial buildings in an enterprise zone can claim an initial allowance of 100%.

Generous tax advantages are available to those who are willing to invest money into commercial property in such designated zones.

A good example of an area that is designated as an enterprise zone is London's docklands.

The main features of EZTs are as follows.

- They have generous tax-saving advantages, where costs of building commercial premises in such areas will qualify for 100% capital allowances that can be offset against taxable income or sometimes against capital gains.

  The capital allowance

  a) for an individual can be set off against any other income of that tax year or the following tax year;

  b) for a company can be set off against any other income or chargeable gains of that accounting period or future accounting periods.

- Businesses do not have to pay business rates as they are offered 'no business rate' deals (rates holidays).
- Rental income can be generated once the commercial property is let.
- Any interest paid on money borrowed from a bank to invest can be offset against any rental income, thereby minimising your tax bill.

28.2. Tax Benefits Associated With EZT?

Here are some tax benefits of using an EZT.

a) The investor can claim a capital allowance that can be used to reduce their income for tax purposes. The initial allowance is equal to 100% of the cost of the commercial property, less the amount paid for the land.

b) The investor can choose to claim as much or as little of the initial capital allowance as they wish. For the individual the loss created by the allowance can be set off against any other income of that tax year or the following tax year, and any remainder can be carried forward to be set off against future rental income.

c) For a company the loss created can be set off against income and chargeable gains of that accounting period or future accounting periods.

Owing to the capital allowance balancing charges rules, if the property is sold before 25 years, there is a claw back of the capital allowances claimed by the investor.

The standard way around this obstacle is for the investor to grant a long-term lease on the property to a purchaser after seven years have expired. Provided the lessor does not have a guaranteed exit arrangement, the claw back will not apply here.

The same treatment applies to the first purchaser of an EZT investment within two years of the first use of the building.

Case Study - 97 : Claiming Tax Relief When Investing in an EZT

Bill has an annual income of £60,000. He invests £50,000 in an EZT, of which 90%, or £45,000, is eligible for claiming as a capital allowance.

£22,500 is claimed in that tax year, and £22,500 is claimed in the next tax year, taking away most of their higher-rate tax liability (~40%). The tax saving is £18,000.

This means that cost of the investment to Bill is £32,000.

28.3. When is It Beneficial to Use an EZT?

EZT investments can be particularly beneficial with gearing.

Consider the following scenario.

Case Study - 98 : Benefit of using an EZT

Suppose you invest £50,000 in an enterprise zone, where £20,000 of the cost is funded from your personal savings, and a loan of £30,000 makes up the remaining amount.

According to the theory, the rental receipts will cover the interest payments to the lender, and the interest payments themselves are a tax-allowable expense that can be set off against the rental receipts in computing the investors tax liability on the rental receipts. The investment of £50,000 has cost the investor a mere £2,000.

The question mark over this, however, is outlined in the following section.

28.4. Disadvantages of EZT

It must be understood that there are definite risks and drawbacks associated with investing in enterprise zone trusts.

These are highlighted below.

a) There is a risk of not being able to rent out the property once it has been developed/built. This means that an investor with a loan will end up having to fund the interest payments from his own pocket.

   However, as always, it is important to make sure you do your research thoroughly before deciding in which area to invest.

b) It may not be so easy to sell just when the investor should choose to do so, especially as he has joined together with others to form a trust to purchase jointly.

c) Buying an EZT property, with the associated tax advantages, may cause the initial purchase price to be artificially inflated.

International Property Taxation

29. Essential Tax Advice for International Property Investors by Daniel Feingold

29.1. About Daniel Feingold

Daniel is a Barrister (Non-Practising) who heads Strategic Tax Planning, a Tax Law Consultancy that has as one of its specialities UK and International Tax Planning for both high net worth individuals and corporate clients. This includes both structuring for UK clients investing in property abroad and UK property acquisitions for foreign investors. His advice is sought after by many accounting and law firms around the UK and overseas.

Daniel has over 22 years experience specialising in tax law since qualifying as a Barrister in July 1983.

He has spent time at the Bar, in several leading City of London law firms and latterly in the International Tax Department of a leading accountancy firm, before establishing his own Tax Consultancy.

Daniel is the lead international tax expert and a technical author for www.property-tax-portal.co.uk.

Daniel has written and lectured extensively on property tax planning; including the pitfalls of Spanish and French property investment and is a regular contributor to several publications on the whole spectrum of tax planning, especially avoiding capital gains on property sales.

Daniel is known as a 'creative' tax expert and has formulated his own unique tax mitigating solutions.

You can learn more about Daniel on-line at the following link:

➔ http://www.property-tax-portal.co.uk/consultancy_daniel.shtml

In the section below Daniel answers the most burning questions international investors have.

29.2. UK People Investing Outside the UK

For anybody investing overseas, what are the five most important tax considerations they need to make?

I would list these as follows:

'How is any capital gain on the property you are going to invest in going to be taxed in that country where you are investing in? Is there a withholding tax (which means that the country where the property is situated requires the purchaser to withhold a percentage of the purchase price and pay it over to the tax authorities?

How is any rental income going to be taxed? Is there a minimum tax on rental income? Is there a withholding tax (which means that the country where you get the rental income from somebody has to pay over a certain amount of tax to their tax authorities first)?

The third most important tax consideration is 'What Inheritance Tax will be levied on death or a gift of the property by the owner in that country where the property is situated? '

The fourth one I would say would be 'Are there any other local taxes to consider such as, purchase taxes when you buy a property, annual rates, (the equivalent of UK rates or council tax), and one that you probably won't have thought of is – annual wealth taxes, which are based on the value of a persons assets situated in that country?

And the fifth is to probably make sure that you know all the tax implications before you sign any legal binding agreement on the property.

If I invest overseas then when and where do I pay income tax?

With regards to income tax you will be liable to pay tax in the country where the property is situated. So for example if you have an investment property in Spain then you will be liable to pay tax in Spain.

It is important to note that you will also be liable to pay income tax in the UK on the rental income; however you will get a credit for any tax that you have to pay in the overseas country.

When does the tax year start and end in overseas countries?

Most overseas countries have a tax year that runs form the 1st January to the 31st December. This is very different to the UK tax year which runs from the 6th April to the 5th April.

What is a double taxation agreement?

These are agreements that are signed between the tax authorities of two separate countries. For example UK and France have a double taxation treaty. The objective of the treaty is to make sure that no income or gains or even other taxes are levied twice on the same portion of income.

So for example if you have a rental income of £10,000 on your property in France, then it should only be subject to income tax once as it would be unfair if this whole amount was taxed again in the UK.

The double taxation agreement also ensures that you do not pay income tax that is greater than what you would pay in the UK.

Double taxation agreements are complex International Tax Treaties and you should seek professional advice about their application.

How can I use double taxation treaties to my advantage?

Well, this is difficult when it comes to property because property income and in fact the capital gains from properties are normally reserved under a double taxation treaty to the country where the property is located.

So it is really quite hard to get a benefit, although sometimes there are areas where for instance a limit can be put on how much tax on rental income can be levied. So for instance there could be a limited taxing right on rental income in the country where the property is, and so there would be a saving or benefit there.

Or they may reserve the right to tax the capital gain to the country to where the person is resident, and there could be a tax saving there.

So there are a few but very limited opportunities where double taxation treaty can work to a person's advantage when investing in property.

My overseas property developer does not provide any tax advice, so should I therefore make it my own responsibility to seek professional advice before I invest or leave it until I decide to sell the property?

Unfortunately, this is an increasingly (and worryingly) growing trend amongst overseas property developers. The fact of the matter is that like any investment you should take advice from the outset, before you invest overseas.

The rush to jump onto the overseas property bandwagon leads to too many people not considering tax implications, until after they have purchased a property. Not only is this approach extremely high risk, but can also be very costly as well!

For example: Many people investing in Spain do not realise that it has a wealth tax. This is a tax on the value on anyone's assets in Spain, and property is off course classed as an asset. This 'wealth tax' is due annually and varies from between 0.2% and 2.5%. The higher the value of your property then the greater tax you will have to pay annually.

Another very common misconception about Spain is that Spanish capital gains tax is reduced on an annual basis so that say after 10 or 15 years of ownership you are not subject to any capital gains tax. This tax break was actually revoked several years ago and replaced with a fixed 35% capital gain for non-residents, but alarmingly developers have been selling properties and advising that there will be no tax liability in 10-15 years time. The good news is that in Spain and following an EU Court ruling the Spanish Government are proposing to reduce this rate from 35% to18% from January 1st 2007. So if you have bought in Spain it maybe worth waiting, but remember this is only a proposal and not yet law!

Can I choose which country I pay tax in? For example the tax rate may be cheaper in the country where I hold my overseas property.

No, not normally. If you are a UK resident and domiciled person (that is somebody who is born and brought up here) you will be liable to UK tax on your worldwide income and capital gains. You will also have to pay income tax and CGT in the country that the property is situated.

However, you need to remember that you will receive a tax credit against your UK tax liability for the tax that you have paid overseas.

Case Study - 99 : Paying tax in two countries

John buys an investment property in Spain for £300,000.

He rents it out for several weeks in the summer and receives £10,000 in rental income. His tenants (or the Spanish agent) should withhold 25% (without any deductions) and pay that over to the Spanish tax authorities as his Spanish tax liability.

In the UK John will be able to deduct the Spanish tax charged at 25% from his UK tax liability charged at 40% (assuming he is a higher rate taxpayer).

John will be able only for UK tax purposes to deduct any expenses in Spain such as agent's fees, repairs and mortgage interest. He may find that he has little or no further UK income tax liability because the Spanish tax has been deducted without taking into account any of these expenses.

There is one other point that is probably worth mentioning for property investors. It may be possible, and this would be subject to advice on which specific country you are investing in, to form a local company and for that company to hold the property.

In such a case you may only have a liability to pay tax on the rental income in that country.

However this is subject to very careful tax planning advice.

If I sell a property abroad and pay the local taxes; I'm only liable for UK Capital gains tax when I bring the money back to the UK – Is that right?

Sadly no, this is a really old chestnut and many people make this mistake.

If you sell a property abroad and even if you have to pay local capital gains tax you are taxed within the UK on your world-wide gains as they arise. So even if you don't bring the money back into the UK, you still have to pay capital gains tax on that money.

If people misunderstand this and leave the money on deposit overseas; then there can be very serious consequences. For instance you could end up paying interest and even penalties to the Inland Revenue if you delay informing them about a capital gain on a property you have sold several years earlier.

I can give you a very good example of how this happens.

Many people sell their overseas properties when they have made a considerable gain. For instance I have many clients who are able to sell their property in Spain totally capital gains tax free because under a special law there, they held the property and they bought it quite a while ago, so they therefore pay no Spanish tax.

They just deposit the money they have received from the property into a bank account in Spain and then they assume that there is nothing more they need to do.

However, it is only when they contact somebody like myself a few years down the line and mention this point that they realise they have a tax problem.

If people have already made this mistake what should they do now?

I would recommend contacting a UK tax adviser who can then inform the UK Inland Revenue and negotiate a settlement on your behalf, at the lowest tax cost.

The longer you leave it the more interest and the higher any penalties will be.

If I sell my apartment abroad and buy a villa, surely I'll be able to rollover the gain I've made into the new villa and therefore I'll only need to pay Capital Gains Tax when I sell that in the future?

I am afraid that this is simply not true.

In the UK the Revenue and Customs view investing in property as an investment and not a business. Roll-over relief is something specific to people who are in business.

For example if you have business premises from where you operate a business and then sell the premises and buy a bigger business premises, then you can roll-over the gain you have made. Now this can't be done with investment property in the UK, and it certainly can't be done with investment property abroad.

However there is one exception to this.

You often find in other tax systems: For example the system in the US, they allow a type of roll-over relief, and people spend a lot of time worrying about this trying to work out if they can get an advantage from it. But there is a problem. Even if the US allows roll-over relief; the UK does not. Therefore because you are taxed in the UK on the gains wherever you make them, if you sell a property in the US and try to use their roll-over relief on the gain you won't be allowed to use it for UK capital gains tax purposes, only for calculating US capital gains. This means that people will expend a lot of energy worrying about foreign roll-over relief when it is not going to affect their UK tax bill as they will still have the same overall liability.

Inheritance Tax overseas on the property is not a worry as I'll leave it to the wife in my will, so there's no tax to pay until she dies?

Unfortunately this is a terribly common misconception.

In UK tax law you have what is called a complete exemption if you leave your property to your spouse. In other words there is no tax to pay at that point.

In most European countries they have a very different approach to the law of inheritance. They have what is called 'Forced Heirship', which means that you have to leave your estate in equal proportions to your children and your wife.

Also there is only a very limited amount for gifts to the spouse and in some case as low as £15,000 and after that you start to pay Inheritance Tax.

So, it is something that causes a lot of people who have gone to live in Spain, or people who have Spanish holiday homes, a lot of problems. This is because they suddenly get a shock when the spouse dies and they assume that there is nothing to pay. They will suddenly get a huge Spanish inheritance tax bill and they really haven't got very much in the way of other liquid assets. This can often force them to sell the property triggering a further problem as they may have to pay capital gains tax as well. So, it can cause a lot of financial problems if this is not planned properly.

It is very important to get your planning right on this by taking local advice. There are ways of getting round this problem by holding properties in a company or creating a debt against the property.

Can I sell my overseas contract and avoid tax?

A year ago I put down a 30% deposit on an 'off plan' apartment in Spain. It will be built in October at which point I will decide whether to get a mortgage and keep it or sell it before completion - at a profit I hope!

Will I have to pay CGT on the profit if I sell the contract without actually owning the property and will I have to declare the transaction to the Inland Revenue?

Many people have been misled concerning the taxation in Spain and the UK of Spanish ' off plan' investments.

In Spain, if you have been registered with the legal title to the property (and your Spanish Lawyer should have done so), then you are selling an interest in Spanish property. Even if you are not, you will still be taxable in Spain, as you are dealing with a contractual right over Spanish property. This is subject to 35% Spanish CGT. I am aware that some Spanish Lawyers are not registering the title and advising that the "off-plan" purchase and sale on can be treated as a *private contract* that is not subject to Spanish tax. Since the Spanish Revenue, the Hacienda started arresting Spanish lawyers and charging them with assisting tax fraud, participating in this strategy could lead to criminal charges in Spain and the Spanish Lawyer will have to give your details to the Hacienda to avoid a prison sentence!

The only possible exception is if you are actually just purchasing a share in some form of foreign investment vehicle outside Spain that owns the Spanish property, (and this would be very risky from a property rights point of view in Spain!).

In Spain, the Purchaser must withhold 5% of the purchase price and pay it over to the Spanish tax authorities.

You then have to file a tax return in Spain and if the 5% is more than the 35% you will be entitled to a repayment.

In the UK you are taxable on your world-wide income and gains. This means that you would get a credit for the 35% Spanish CGT and would, if you are a higher rate taxpayer, owe a further 5% to the Inland Revenue here, to make it up to 40%. You need to declare the gain here to claim credit for the Spanish tax paid.

In the event that you do not pay Spanish tax, you would then simply have to pay 40% in the UK.

If I invest overseas, which tax authority needs to be notified that I own property? In other words do I need to inform the tax authorities in the UK and the overseas tax authority?

Assuming that there is rental income generated, then both tax authorities need to be informed. If you only buy a holiday home that is not rented, then initially only the tax authority in the country where the property is situated.

However, it is likely that sooner or later you will need to inform the UK Revenue & Customs as well.

29.3. Tax Advice for Ex-Pats

If I leave the UK to live and work in another country, but rent out my UK residence then am I liable to pay income tax?

Yes you have to pay UK income tax on your rental income. The amount paid can actually be up to the highest rate of UK income tax, which is currently 40%.

Furthermore there is an obligation on the tenant, i.e. the person who has rented the property or on the estate agent who is handling the rental agreement, to withhold 22% of the gross rent from any money they pay over to you overseas.

There is a way out of this by having an agreement with the Inland Revenue. Such an agreement is the **Non Resident Landlord Scheme**. Once an agreement is reached with them, the rental income money can be paid to you (i.e. the landlord) without making the 22% deduction / commission.

Just to clarify if you have a Non Resident Landlord agreement then you would pay the tax on the usual dates under the self-assessment tax return. In order words you must declare the rent on your tax return and pay any tax due.

The other point to remember is that you may also have a tax liability on that rental income in the foreign country, where you have gone to live. Again, you will receive a credit for any UK tax you pay. However you will have an additional tax liability depending on the rules in that country.

If I leave the UK to retire abroad or live abroad permanently, what income tax and capital gains tax implications are there for my UK properties?

Firstly, you are still technically liable to pay income tax on your rental property profits. This often comes as a shock to many people. The reason why this is quite shocking to people is that some many believe that if you leave the UK and go and live abroad you are going to save UK tax. In fact, as far as rental income on property there is no saving whatsoever. E.g. if your rental income makes you a higher rate taxpayer you will have to pay UK income tax at 40%.

Secondly, capital gains tax will also be due if you decide to sell your UK properties once you have gone abroad. It is vital that you don't sell the properties until the tax year following the year in which you leave. So for example if you left the UK in January 2006 you cannot sell that property until after April 6th 2006.

Why can I not sell till April 6th 2006?

This is because the Inland Revenue do not split tax years for capital gains or in fact income tax. If you are resident in the UK for anytime after 6th April you are theoretically resident for the wholes tax year. They only waive this rule by a special concession, which is only really applicable for income and gains on earnings and assets acquired after you leave the UK.

Do I have to pay UK Capital Gains Tax if I sell my UK property?

If you leave the UK permanently for at least five full tax years, starting from April 6th, then there is no UK Capital Gains Tax on selling the UK properties.

If you do return within that period, then you will have to pay the UK Capital Gains Tax.

Does this mean that I cannot return to the UK at all for the entire five years?

No, you can come back for up to 90 days on average over 4 UK tax years. Up to 182 days; if you are protected by a double tax treaty with your new country of residence (please note for this I am referring to returning to the UK and becoming treated as resident here).

Someone told me I could still have to pay Capital Gains tax in the Country where I'm going to live on my UK properties is that true?

Depending on the specific rules of each country, you may well have a tax liability there. Spain has 15% capital gains for residents going up to 18% on January 1st 2007. Some countries have generous tax rules that only tax gains from the date of taking up residence there. So if you sell within a short period of arrival and the property hasn't gone up there is no capital gains tax there.

Other countries tax the property anyway subject to Capital Gains Tax. In this situation you would be liable to pay tax subject to normal UK CGT rules.

This is a vital area people need to get advice on before they go to a location to know what they face in terms of taxation.

Case Study - 100 : CGT when leaving the UK (1)

Jim leaves the UK and goes to live in Canada. His investment properties are worth £250,000 on leaving on April 5th 2004. In July 2004, three months after leaving the UK, he sells for £260,000. Only £10,000 is subject to Canadian CGT.

Case Study - 101 : CGT when leaving the UK (2)

Sally leaves the UK and goes to live in Spain on April 5th 2004. Her investment properties are worth £200,000. In December 2004 she sells for £200,000. Her acquisition cost was £120,000 in 2002 and she pays Spanish CGT @15% (approximately £12,000) on an £80,000 gain minus a small inflation allowance.

How long am I treated as UK Domiciled, when I leave the UK to live somewhere else?

This is a complex question because it involves understanding what **Domicile** means.

Domicile basically means the country whose laws you choose to be governed by and where you consider your permanent home. If you leave the UK, sell all your properties and sever most of your connections with the UK, then you could theoretically be a Domicile in another country within a few years.

However there is an inheritance tax rule called **Deemed Domicile** which will basically tax you on your world wide assets in the UK, at the end of the 4th tax year after leaving the UK.

So, even if you can move abroad permanently and sever sufficient connections with the UK and build up enough connections with your new country, you will still be subject to UK inheritance tax on your worldwide assets until the end of the 4th tax year after leaving the UK.

There are some double tax treaties that can override this rule, but they require specialist advice.

Is it true that my UK assets such as UK property will still be subject to UK Inheritance Tax, even if I'm considered Domiciled in another Country?

Yes, as well as having the Deemed Domicile rule, which keeps you in the UK inheritance tax net after you have left the UK, the UK subjects any property in the UK to inheritance tax. This is on the basis that it is situated in the UK. It actually doesn't matter where the person who owns it is Domiciled.

The only relevant test is where the property is.

Is there anyway of avoiding my UK inheritance Tax liability whilst I'm still Deemed Domiciled and Domiciled abroad if I keep my UK property?

Yes.

There are some measures you can put into place even during the Deemed Domiciled period to actually convert UK property, and any other assets you may have, into a special kind of property called **excluded property**.

This is too complicated to explain here but it is suffice to say that this is a solution.

One other method that people look at when they are Domiciled abroad is to sell, or to transfer, their UK property to a non UK company and/or Trust. By doing this they can remove it from the UK tax 'net'. However Stamp Duty and the new Pre-Owned Asset Tax rules for inheritance tax need to be taken into account.

In the 2006-2007 tax year each individual has a UK inheritance tax allowance of £285,000.

Another simple planning method would be to gift a share in any UK property to your wife and children. By doing this you multiply the £285,000 allowance a number of times by the people in whose name you have the property. This will create a UK inheritance tax liability for seven years from the date of any gifts or transfers. However this strategy requires specific advice.

What are your top three tax saving tips for Ex-pats?

Firstly, you should appoint a UK agent and apply to be taxed under the Non Resident Landlord scheme (NRL). This is essential if you want to avoid the 22% withholding tax.

Secondly, you need to consider ways to minimise the tax on UK rental income and avoid hitting the high tax bracket. You could again give a share of property to your wife or children, because each individual will then have UK rental income and will have the benefit of the personal allowance and also the lower tax bands. This can be a very valuable opportunity to save tax and avoid the 40% rate.

Thirdly, you need to establish how the rental income in the UK is to be taxed in the new country where you are re-locating. You need to know if it is going to be taxed in a beneficial way for you or whether you will be better off using an offshore or home country company.

29.4. Tax considerations for people investing in the UK

For overseas investors, what tax considerations should they make before investing in the UK?

First and foremost an overseas investor must get UK tax advice before they get to the exchange of contracts on any UK property. In other words, get appropriate tax advice before any legally binding documents are signed.

As a general rule, I would say that holding property in the UK in your own name is generally unattractive for tax reasons and it's far better to hold it through an off shore company. If you find this out too late and you have already exchanged contracts, it can be very costly to then sell that property on, or transfer it on to an off shore company - especially from a UK stamp duty perspective.

When does an overseas investor become liable to UK tax?

An overseas investor would be liable to UK tax from the point where they generate a rental income profit.

Again, it is back to the point I mentioned earlier with UK ex-pats, 22% tax would be withheld or ought to be withheld on the rent.

The investor needs to register for the Non Resident Landlord Scheme.

If the property has been bought in their own name then they could be liable to UK tax of 40%.

What can I do to minimise UK tax on rental income?

Form an off shore company.

Under the UK tax law any non-UK Company owning property in the UK can only be taxed on rental income with a maximum of 22%.

If the company has to take out a loan to acquire the property, then it is entitled to deduct the interest on that loan. The rules are such that you can actually loan your own money to your off shore company and get a deduction from that.

What can I do to make sure my Profit on selling a property is treated as a Capital Gain and therefore tax-free?

To guarantee a UK property is not going to be subject to UK capital gains tax it must be held as a pure investment.

A non-resident investing in UK property will not be subject to UK capital gains tax unless the property has been re-furbished or developed in any way. A property must be held as an investment for at least one year, so that there is at least one-year's rental income. Please note that this one-year rule is not derived from any official ruling. It is just a rule that has been developed by experience from practitioners dealings with the Inland Revenue on this issue.

Case Study - 102 : Non-UK residents selling UK property

Alice is resident in Barbados. She decides to buy an investment property in London. The property is purchased for £250,000 and she rents it out at £2,000 per month. She holds the property for two years and then decides to sell it for £300,000.

She will not be liable to pay any UK capital gains tax as the property was held purely for investment purposes.

So as an overseas investor, I'm not liable for UK Capital Gains Tax when I sell my investment property, am I?

This is broadly correct.

However it is vital that the property has been held for investment and there has been no significant development work. Again we come back to having at least one-year rental income and also not carrying out any significant development on the property.

If there was significant development on it then there is a potential that the gain could be taxed as UK income so it could be taxed at up to 40%.

Is it true as an overseas investor that I am liable for UK Inheritance Tax on my UK properties?

Yes I am afraid that this is back to the rule in UK tax laws where inheritance tax is levied on the basis of where the property is situated.

A property in the UK held by an overseas investor will still be subject to UK inheritance tax.

Is there a simple way to avoid UK Inheritance Tax?

Yes.

The key rule is that you should not hold a property directly (i.e. in your own personal name) but you should invest via a non-UK (possibly an off shore) company whose share register is kept outside the UK.

If this is the case then there is no UK inheritance tax on the asset. This is because it is held in a foreign company and the asset that you hold are actually foreign company shares. This means that the shares are not classed as UK property.

This will therefore allow you to keep the asset outside of the UK inheritance tax net.

As an overseas investor, I've been offered the chance to invest in a UK property development. Is the taxation any different? Surely, I'm not liable to UK Capital Gains and so the profits are UK tax-free?

The minute you move from just buying a property to hold as an investment to carrying out development work or trading, buying & selling property then, there is a risk that you can be taxed in the UK with income tax up to 40%.

This is a very complex area and it involves special anti avoidance provision in UK tax law.

If someone was considering not just investing in the UK but participating in a UK development then there are two planning measures they should look in to.

First of all, by using double taxation treaties with various locations it may be possible to avoid the potential application of this section and ensure that any profits on the property are treated as capital gains and not taxable in the UK.

Another simple tip in this area is that if there is substantial risk that you are going to carry out some development in a property then you might want to consider involving a UK company and letting that company pay tax on the development gains. If you do this then you will be outside the scope of the special anti avoidance provision.

Also, if the company is making profits up to £300,000 in the UK then it is only going to be subject to corporation tax at 19%, which represents a considerable saving on income tax of 40%.

29.5. Location Focus - Spain

What tax advice do you have for people who invest in Spain?

Spain is a very popular location to invest in, but unfortunately a lot of people I find don't look into the Spanish tax implications of what they are doing until they have actually bought a property.

The first point to remember is that when you purchase a new property in Spain there is value added tax (VAT) on that transaction. VAT in Spain is called IVA and is chargeable at about 7% at the moment.

The second point to note is that if you have received rental income from a Spanish property then you are going to be paying Spanish tax at 25% on that rental income.

However, remember that you can credit that 25% tax against your UK tax liability. This means that if you are a basic rate UK taxpayer and pay tax at a rate of 22% then you can't claim the 3% tax difference. However if you are a higher rate (40%) tax-payer then you will need to pay the additional 15% in the UK.

It is also important to understand that you cannot claim the usual deductions for the cost of any repairs, agency fees, mortgage interest etc., against the 25% withholding tax as you can in the UK.

Spain also has an annual wealth tax, which is a tax on the value of anyone's assets. For a non-resident this is limited to the assets that are within Spain.

If you purchase a Spanish property that is an asset then the wealth tax due will vary from 0.2% to 2.5%.

It is really only when you are purchasing multi-million pound properties that you would be paying the 2.5% rate. If for example the value of your Spanish property was 200,000 Euros then the taxable rate would approximately be .22%. Although this would appear to be a modest tax it is an annual tax. This means that it is due every single year and as the property increases, then so will the taxable rate and the amount you pay.

There is also another tax that is due, which is the equivalent the UK's rates or council tax. This is also due annually.

A very important aspect for investors is the taxation of capital gains.

In Spain, capital gains made by a non-resident are taxed at a rate of 35%. This should be reduced to 18% from January 1st 2007 if passed into law in Spain. This may seem unfair as they only tax their own residents at 15%. This has been levied as a result of widespread Spanish tax evasion by people using offshore companies. Therefore it is essential to carry out some tax planning before you invest in Spain.

One of the common misconceptions is that Spanish capital gains tax is reduced on an annual basis after a certain number of years. Many people believe that if they hold onto their investment property for 10 or 15 years then they will get a complete exemption. This ruling was revoked several years ago but there are a lot of people who have been sold properties by developers and have been told that after 10 or 15 years there is no Spanish capital gains tax. This is not true and the rate is 35%.

Also, under Spanish law the purchaser is obliged to withhold 5% of the agreed price and pay that to the Spanish tax authority on account of the vendor's liability for Spanish capital gains tax. Please note that this is not 5% of the gain. It is actually 5% of the sale price. The purchaser has to pay this tax over to the Spanish tax authorities immediately.

Finally, I want to get on to something which people keep forgetting about, and this is Spanish Inheritance Tax.

In Spain there are several regions, which are referred to as autonomous regions, e.g. the area of Andalusia. In some of these regions they tried to abolish inheritance tax and give generous exceptions. Again many people are being misguided by Spanish developers and agents out there, and are being told about these generous exemptions.

Spanish inheritance tax in localised regions like Andalusia, which are being introduced and widened each year do not apply to non residents of Spain. This means that a UK investor holding property in Spain directly in their own name is subject to the Spanish inheritance tax.

Spanish inheritance tax works on a basis of how 'close' the inheriting relative is to you. So for a wife and children there is one rate and the further the more distant you get away the higher the tax liability. For example if you are not legally married to your partner and are just a common law spouse, then you will be taxed at a very high rate.

One final point to note is that there is a very small exemption for gifts left to the spouse in Spain.

If you are investing in Spain, as a non-resident property owner, you could be liable for the following taxes:

Spanish Property Tax

Tax On Rental Income

Rental income is subject to 25% of gross rents without any deductions.

Wealth Tax

Spanish Wealth tax is levied on Spanish Assets of non-residents without any exempt amount.

Spanish residents enjoy a nil band of more than Euro 100,000!

So, any value of Spanish property will be subject to at least .2% and up to 2.5% wealth tax (although this latter rate kicks in at over Euro 10 million.). This is added to the rental income tax and paid at the same time.

Capital Gains Tax (CGT)

This is a shock for most non-residents, as the rate for Spanish residents is only 15%! For non-residents its 35% changing to 18% form January 1st 2007 if passed into law. and the worrying news is that under Spanish tax law the purchaser must withhold 5% of the purchase price and pay it to the tax authorities on account of this tax.

You then have to make a repayment claim, if this is higher than the actual gain.

Inheritance Tax (IHT)

This tax is levied based on the relationship of the beneficiary to the deceased.

For a Spouse, there is an exempt amount of just Euro 16,000 and then tax at progressive rates from 7.65%- 34%. For unmarried beneficiaries such as girlfriends and friends, there is NO EXEMPT amount.

Comments

High Spanish capital gains and exorbitant inheritance tax rates for surviving spouses and unmarried partners mean planning is essential. This may involve using a UK or Spanish Company, holding the property as joint owners, or taking out life insurance.

The failure to plan for Spanish taxes often leads to taxes so high that the property has to be sold to pay them.

29.6. Location Focus – France

What tax advice do you have for people who invest in France?

French property taxation is in some ways similar to Spanish taxation, but it has its own idiosyncrasies and differences.

If you are going to purchase a property or investment in France there is some good news and some bad news. This is because there have been some very recent changes in French tax law.

The first is that there is a simplified system where you can elect to have a fixed tax rate applied to your rental income. This is called **micro-bic**.

Otherwise the micro-bic is basically a notional rental income attributed to your property with six deductions. The alternative to micro-bic is to submit proper figures as you would in any other location with your actual deductions for mortgage interest, repairs, etc. The rental income is subject to 25% tax for non-residents, which is very similar to Spain, except it allows for deductions.

Again with France you must remember that there are taxes on purchase which are similar to those in Spain.

The next aspect is French capital gains tax. Now there has been some very good news on this front which is probably going to make France a good place to invest if you're worried about foreign capital gains tax.

As opposed to the 35% which is levied in Spain, in France they have a system which now differentiates between residents of other EU countries such as UK and non EU residents. If you are a resident of the UK then the maximum French capital gains tax rate is 16%.

In addition to this, they offer some generous deductions from the capital gain which are fixed but are quite useful. Also, if you hold a property for more than 5 years then the capital gain is reduced from 5th until the 15th year at 10% per annum. So after holding a property for 15 years, there is no capital gains tax due at all in France.

Now, I just want to mention at this point that there is a distinction in France between what you might call mature or professional property investors. If people in France register as a professional property investor, (which would normally mean they have got quite a significant number of properties generating a fairly large rental income), they can probably be exempt from French capital gains tax after just 5 years.

Again just like Spain, France has a system of inheritance tax which is not like the UK.

However there is a spouse exemption and it is more generous than the Spanish one and there is an exemption for gifts left to the wife. After this the rates rise up to an overall rate of 40%, again depending on the connection of the person inheriting to the person leaving the property. The rates can rise up to 60%.

Therefore it is important to know that when you are buying a property in France and want to get round the French Inheritance Tax Rules that you don't exclude either your wife or children from your estate. French inheritance tax rules are based on the concept of forced heirship, which means you must leave reasonable proportion to your wife and any children.

You also have to look at the way you are going to hold property in France. There is a concept very similar to holding a property as joint tenants in the UK where on the death of the first spouse the other spouse inherits. This can produce tax savings and is called **en tontine**. However this does not work in every case and on transfer there is 4.8% transfer tax to pay.

By far the best way to hold French property for married couples is under a **marriage contract**. This treats the property as community property and there is no tax on transfer on death or otherwise between the spouses.

Another very popular method of investing in French property is to hold French property in a special kind of company called an SCI or **Society Civil Immobiliere**. This is a specific company that is used for holding property and you can transfer the shares of the company under UK law and avoid any of the French inheritance tax complications.

However, it does have some potential UK complications. So, before anybody rushes out to form one of these companies it is important you take specific advice. This is because there can be potential UK tax problems if you are going to be a director or will be running the French property company.

If you are investing in France, as a non-resident property owner, you could be liable for the following taxes:

French Property Tax

Tax On Rental Income

There a number of regimes for taxing the income from French rentals. For furnished property there is the MICRO-BIC. This tax offers a deduction of a flat 72% for expenses on income up to approximately Euro 76,000 with the remainder taxed at 25%.

On income above that, you can only operate on an actual basis. This is very generous, but it plays havoc with UK tax liabilities as the MICRO-BIC deduction is not allowable and the income has to be calculated on an actual basis.

Again, unfurnished property income up to Euro 15,000 can benefit from MICRO-FONCIERS that allows 60% flat rate deduction and the remainder taxed at 25%. Above that sum the actual basis is used and again, for UK purposes a separate calculation will be needed.

It is therefore best for most UK Taxpayers to use the actual basis and pay 25% flat rate French tax and get a credit against your UK. The exceptions would be where the rental income is in a basic rate taxpayers name paying UK tax at 22%.

Wealth Tax

If you have French assets over Euro 785,000 then there is an annual wealth tax at rates of .55% to 1.8%.

This applies to all French assets of non-residents, including bank accounts and property.

If this is an issue, there are planning measures to reduce this that can be taken especially by the creation of debts which are deductible

Capital Gains Tax (CGT)

For EU Residents capital gains are chargeable at 16% for property held for 2 years or more.

For property held for less than 2 years, there is usually income tax chargeable at the normal rates which for 2006 go up to approximately 40%.

For property held for 5 years or more, there is a further annual deduction of 10% of the gain until after 15 years or more of ownership. After that, there are no Capital Gains to pay whatsoever.

It is also important to note that a Professional Landlord of furnished property taxable under the MICRO-BIC or on an actual basis is not subject to capital gains after 5 years of ownership.

Inheritance Tax (IHT)

French Inheritance Tax is levied in progressive bands.

The rates then depend on who the property is left with, Spouses and close relatives paying at rates of up to 40%.

If the property is left to an unmarried partner or friend, the rates go up to 60% with a tax-free allowance of only Euro 1,500!

Comments

French income and capital gains taxes are generally lower than UK Rates and so do not present much of a problem for investors, unless they are going in for "OFF-

PLAN" or other short-term investments that they will hold for less than 2 years.

French Inheritance Tax is much more of a problem and advanced planning is vital before the property is purchased. This can take the form of holding the property either EN TONTINE, a form of joint ownership, or under a MARRIAGE CONTRACT arrangement and through either a UK Company or a special type of French Company known as a "SOCIETE CIVILE IMMOBLIERE".

Specialist advice needs to be taken as to the benefits and pitfalls of using each particular method.

29.7. Summary

Is there on final point you would like to make?

I really believe that from my experience too many people invest abroad and get very emotionally involved with the idea of purchasing a property abroad. They don't look into the tax aspects or any other relevant aspects before they go ahead.

Very often there are either other locations where you can buy a property with far less tax complications, or there is planning you can do before you buy a property.

In many cases it may be worthwhile considering buying a property not through your own name but through a company- either a local company in Spain or for instance a local company in France such as the Society Civil Immobliere (SCI).

It might also be worth considering using a UK company. There is no one simple or stock solution and everyone's objectives, family circumstances etc have to be considered.

My key advice would be factor in as part of your purchase the investment in specific tailored tax advice before you buy a property. This is because once the property is registered in your name, it is much harder to do any tax planning.

Good Accountants Do Save You TAX!

30. Finding an Accountant

There is a saying, "a good accountant pays for him/herself". Never a truer word has been spoken but then you have to ask yourself, "How do I find a good accountant?"

In this chapter we will become familiar with and understand how to acquire the services of an excellent accountant.

30.1. Accountants Qualifications

The first step is to ensure that your accountant is a member of a recognised institute.

Some of the popular ones amongst accountants are ACA, ACCA, ICAEW, ICAS etc.

Here is what these abbreviations stand for:

- Association of Chartered Accountants (ACA)
- Association of Chartered Certified Accountants (ACCA)
- Institute of Chartered Accountants in England and Wales (ICAEW)
- Institute of Chartered Accountants in Scotland (ICAS)

Furthermore it would not be a bad idea to pick an accountant who is a member of the Chartered Institute of Taxation or Association of Taxation Technicians.

Getting to know the history of your proposed accountant is a very good idea, so look for the following signs:

a) Are they a former Tax Inspector?
b) Have they passed the Taxation (ATII, ATT) exams?

A qualified tax advisor is useful for all sorts of tax related services and these include:

- Preparing tax returns
- Sole trader tax returns
- Tax planning advice

It is most likely that your tax advisor will charge on an hourly basis. However some will agree a flat fee beforehand.

It is pertinent to ask whether one should go for a general or specialist tax advisor, although it may seem better to go with the general advisor as he/she will most definitely be cheaper.

However in the long-term the specialist may save you money because of his/her in depth knowledge and experience.

30.2. The difference between a general advisor and a tax specialist?

A specialist will have the answer, usually to hand, whereas a non specialist may have to consult Inland Revenue documentation or may indeed consult the specialist and then pass the charge back on to you.

Cost can be a significant issue as a specialist can charge around £270 per hour. For this you get about 15 minutes of quizzing followed by 45 minutes worth of (in most cases) written response (Oh and that's plus VAT!)

To put that into perspective a non specialist can charge around £150 per hour. A typical session with a non specialist can take up to 2.5 hours. This time would be typically spent in the following way:

- 15 minutes of clarification.
- 1.5 hours of research.
- 45 minutes of written response.

As you can see sometimes it is beneficial if you go direct to a specialist, particularly if your questions to your accountant require him/her to study before responding.

With the above two examples in mind it is important to ascertain a working relationship with your advisor. You should be familiar with his/her area of expertise and know what their limitations are i.e. what they are not too hot on.

30.3. Three golden rules for finding a good accountant

30.3.1. Know your investment/business goals

Do you want to buy one or two properties, let them and hold for the long-term or wait for the market to rise and sell? Another scenario is to buy, renovate and sell. What are *your* plans? Knowing these will reflect heavily on what kind of tax advisor you are looking for.

30.3.2. 'Phone a friend'

There is nothing like a personal recommendation!

Do you know of any successful business people? If yes then ask them who there accountant is? Another way to get to know an accountant without paying for it is via your local press. Sometimes local accountants write articles for the local press on a weekly basis.

Also try your solicitor, maybe he/she knows a good accountant.

30.3.3. Drill your accountant

Remember you are the employer, so why not interview your accountant before hiring their services.

Here are some questions that you should put to them:

- *What experiences does the accountant have in your line of work*
- *Does the accountant have clients who will provide a testimonial for him/her*
- *Ask for a free initial consultation so you can assess his/her level of expertise.*
- *How easy is it to get hold of him/her? For example if you have a burning question can you just pick up the phone or do you have to arrange a meeting.*

Are you of a similar age? If you are 28 and your accountant is 50 then when your empire has grown and you are 48 who is going to be your accountant?

- *Does the accountant's knowledge match your goals and intentions?*

Get a clear understanding of his/her costs.

Make sure you understand the relationship you have with your accountant. For example is he/she going to charge you every time you have a question to ask? How easily can you contact him i.e. can you phone him/her anytime or do you always have to book an actual appointment to go and see him/her?

Tax Investigations

31. Getting to Grips with Tax Investigations

The following section is written by Ian McTernan, author of the guide 'How to use companies to cut your property tax bills.' Ian is a specialist in advising and dealing with tax investigations.

I personally deal with a lot of enquiries and am frequently asked by other professionals to handle tax investigations into their clients' affairs.

This is a specialist area that I am very familiar with, and the most important thing I can tell you on the subject is this:

If the Revenue write to you or otherwise contact you about opening an enquiry into your tax return or accounts, seek professional advice straight away.

It still amazes me that people would rather save a few hundred pounds on professional fees and attempt to handle this sort of matter themselves rather than seeking professional advice before doing anything.

This approach leads to people getting themselves into all sorts of problems and stress!

Presentation and phraseology are very important in answering Revenue questions, and it is generally accepted within the profession that on no account should clients be allowed to talk with or otherwise deal with the Revenue during the course of an enquiry.

This is not because we think clients are thick or don't know what they are doing. I have handled an investigation into a firm of accountants' accounts, and the senior partner there managed to throw a huge spanner in the works by deciding he wanted to speed things up by talking to the inspector handling the case.

There is nothing worse than finding out that the client has phoned the Revenue back in response to a Revenue call and just shot themselves in the foot.

REMEMBER: The Revenue will try to establish the worst possible scenario for the client in order to maximise their tax take and justify having opened an enquiry in the first place.

By contacting the client, they can get the client to admit to something which could be completely incorrect, but once the client has told them what he thought was correct, it is then very difficult to persuade the Revenue that they have misunderstood matters.

31.1. Types of Enquiries/Investigations

Most enquiries opened by the Revenue are **aspect enquiries**.

These enquiries are where the Revenue wants more detail about a particular entry in a return.

More thorough enquiries are dealt with as **full enquiries**, where the entire year will be put under review and all aspects of the return will be checked for accuracy.

There are also investigations carried out by various other branches of the Revenue, such as the **Special Compliance Office (SCO)**, which usually handle larger cases and cases where criminal prosecution is being contemplated by the Revenue.

31.2. How to Cut Your Chances of Being Investigated

So what can you do to cut down on your chances of an enquiry and to ensure that your returns are correct?

Firstly, and most importantly, ensure that full records are kept for every entry in your tax return.

This means keeping every single

- credit card slip;
- email confirmation (of purchases);
- sales receipt;
- rent book;
- contract and rental agreement.

These *must* be kept for a minimum of 5 years and 10 months from the end of the year of assessment to which they relate.

The Revenue has the power to enquire into tax years up to six years after that year has passed. This is provided they find an error in the tax return for the current or previous year within the time limits imposed by the legislation.

Using other powers, they can extend their assessment of under-declared income to up to 20 years where fraudulent activity is suspected.

31.3. How the Inland Revenue Can Find Out About You

Here are some of the techniques the Inland Revenue use to find people for investigation.

- **Potluck**
  The Revenue selects a certain number of cases to make aspect enquiries into on a purely random basis, so you could just be unlucky.

- **Third-party informers**
  The Revenue will select cases based on third-party information.
  For example, this can include a tenant informing the Revenue of the amount of rental income they pay when making a claim for tax credits or social security payments.

  The Revenue will then link up the records and discover that the landlord has not made any return of any rental income ever or a much lower gross rent figure is shown on their return than that quoted by the tenant.

- **Some people are just never satisfied!**

The Revenue also read local advertisements taken out by traders, landlords, etc., and try to link these with known taxpayers. This was a favourite pastime of one particular inspector I knew and one that proved very lucrative for the Revenue! (Probably not as lucrative for the dodging taxpayers though!)

- **New stamp duty and land tax returns**
  With the new stamp duty land tax returns, the Revenue will soon build up a powerful database to supplement the information held at the Land Registry so that they can find out who owns more than one property. They will also be able to track sales and purchases. Anyone who thinks that they are currently 'getting away with it' better think again!

- **Fact-finding missions**
  Another favourite trick of the Revenue is to discover that you own a second property and do not live there and then wait until the year in which you sell it and fail to notify them of the gain on the property.

  Or better yet, you declare the gain. They will then send you an innocuous-sounding letter asking if there is anything else you need to declare and can you confirm that your return is complete and correct?

  Once you answer yes, they will then inform you that they are opening an investigation as they have information that leads them to believe that you have omitted something from your return.

  They will invite you to declare any omitted income. At this stage, some people will realise the game is up and come clean, but surprisingly, many people think that the Revenue is still 'fishing' and will attempt not to reveal all.

  Imagine the taxpayer's surprise when after denying everything the Revenue finally reveals that they know you sold the property and it has had a variety of people registered to vote at it and on the Council Tax list, but none of them were you! Typically, it is at this late stage that I am contacted and deal with the Revenue, trying to ensure that the client's position is presented in the best possible light with a view to minimising the amount of penalties that the Revenue will seek to impose. Given the client's previous denials, the penalty addition is likely to be quite high. Penalties can be up to 100% of the tax charged, plus interest, so you could face a bill up to 100% of the income you received in the first place.

- **Computers and statistics**
  The Revenue has another tool in their armoury, and this is the **statistics** they have built up as a result of the self-assessment system and the computerisation of records.

  They now hold a database of several hundred thousand records for any type of trade or business, and they have programmed their computers to automatically flag for enquiry any entries in a return that fall outside the statistical norm.

  It is a closely guarded secret as to exactly how far out from the norm you have to be to trigger this, but I am aware of a case that involved 20 mini-cab drivers (I did not deal with this case). They thought they were being clever when they got as many petrol receipts as possible from a local garage and included huge amounts of petrol in their accounts, thereby cutting down their tax bills. Imagine their surprise when each and every one of them was told that they were under enquiry, and on the basis of the amount of petrol they had claimed in their accounts, they must have under-declared their income by about half! Eventually, the case was settled, and every one of them had to pay several thousand pounds in additional tax, interest, and penalties.

If your statistics fall outside the boundaries, such as too much expense of a certain type or too little income for the property concerned, then you are significantly more at risk of having an enquiry aimed at you.

31.4. What If I Do Get Investigated?

If you do have an enquiry, the first thing the inspector will usually ask for is all the records relating to the aspect under enquiry. In the case of rental income, this will include your personal bank statements, credit card statements, all receipts, and anything that has a remote connection to the receipt of the income. So, if you were only declaring one lot of rental income and had two, the Revenue will spot this from the entries on your bank statements!

To cut down on the necessity of having to provide personal bank statements, it is usually a good idea to set up a separate bank account to handle everything to do with the rental properties. Designate one of your credit cards exclusively for use in connection with the properties, and keep good records of all expenses and income. There are fines of up to £3,000 for failure to keep records, and the Revenue are looking for some test cases as I write this—**don't be one of them!**

Why not consider using our innovative and unique property tax management software to keep a documented record of your property income/expenditure and calculate your tax?

Please visit http://www.property-tax-portal.co.uk for more information.

Of course, setting up and running the properties through a limited company will force a lot of good disciplines on you. If you do this, you will need a separate bank account, a credit card taken out in the company name, and accounts drawn up by a professional.

Please note that it is not now necessary to have audited accounts for turnovers of less than £2.8m. At the time of writing, it is soon due to be raised to £5.6m. If your turnover goes above this, then you will have to appoint auditors to do the accounts for you, which will cost considerably more.

Some final advice!
If there is any possibility that you think the Revenue are going to open an enquiry or open an investigation on you or your company, seek professional advice as soon as possible.

Do not respond to the Revenue as this may cause your professional adviser untold headaches and massively increase the fees charged in digging you out of an even bigger hole.

If you don't take professional advice from the outset and decide to handle it yourself, it may just be the most costly decision you ever make.

Finally, remember that tax evasion is a crime and you can be sent to jail for quite a long time, even if you didn't realise you were doing anything wrong. Ignorance is no defence.

Congratulations – You've now finished 'Pay Less Property Tax - 2007'

To learn even more ways on how to legitimately cut your property tax bills please visit: www.property-tax-portal.co.uk.

Appendix

Appendix A—Indexation Factors for Calculating Indexation Relief

	Month											
Year	Jan	Feb	Mar	Apr	May	Jun	Jul	Aug	Sep	Oct	Nov	Dec
1982			1.047	1.006	0.992	0.987	0.986	0.985	0.987	0.977	0.967	0.971
1983	0.968	0.960	0.956	0.929	0.921	0.917	0.906	0.898	0.889	0.883	0.876	0.871
1984	0.872	0.865	0.859	0.834	0.828	0.823	0.825	0.808	0.804	0.793	0.788	0.789
1985	0.783	0.769	0.752	0.716	0.708	0.704	0.707	0.703	0.704	0.701	0.695	0.693
1986	0.689	0.683	0.681	0.665	0.662	0.663	0.667	0.662	0.654	0.652	0.638	0.632
1987	0.626	0.620	0.616	0.597	0.596	0.596	0.597	0.593	0.588	0.580	0.573	0.574
1988	0.574	0.568	0.562	0.537	0.531	0.525	0.524	0.507	0.500	0.485	0.478	0.474
1989	0.465	0.454	0.448	0.423	0.414	0.409	0.408	0.404	0.395	0.384	0.372	0.369
1990	0.361	0.353	0.339	0.300	0.288	0.283	0.282	0.269	0.258	0.248	0.251	0.252
1991	0.249	0.242	0.237	0.222	0.218	0.213	0.215	0.213	0.208	0.204	0.199	0.198
1992	0.199	0.193	0.189	0.171	0.167	0.167	0.171	0.171	0.166	0.162	0.164	0.168
1993	0.179	0.171	0.167	0.156	0.152	0.153	0.156	0.151	0.146	0.147	0.148	0.146
1994	0.151	0.144	0.141	0.128	0.124	0.124	0.129	0.124	0.121	0.120	0.119	0.114
1995	0.114	0.107	0.102	0.091	0.087	0.085	0.091	0.085	0.080	0.085	0.085	0.079
1996	0.083	0.078	0.073	0.066	0.063	0.063	0.067	0.062	0.057	0.057	0.057	0.053
1997	0.053	0.049	0.046	0.040	0.036	0.032	0.032	0.026	0.021	0.019	0.019	0.016
1998	0.019	0.014	0.011									

Appendix B – List of Tax Saving Case Studies

Printed in the United Kingdom
by Lightning Source UK Ltd.
113916UKS00001B/5-82

9 780954 934774